The
Mindfulness
Bible

The
Mindfulness
Bible

Dr Patrizia Collard

The Complete Guide to Living in the Moment

WALKING
STICK
PRESS

Published in the U.S. by Walking Stick Press, an imprint of F+W Media, Inc.
10151 Carver Road, Suite #200, Blue Ash, OH 45242
(800) 289-0963

First published in Great Britain in 2015 by Godsfield Press,
a division of Octopus Publishing Group Ltd, Carmelite House,
50 Victoria Embankment
London EC4Y 0DZ

www.octopusbooks.co.uk

Disclaimer
The author and publisher disclaim to any person or entity, any liability, loss or damage caused or alleged to be caused, directly or indirectly as a result of the use, application or interpretation of any of the contents of this book. All information and/or advice given in this book should not take the place of any medical, counselling, legal, or financial advice given to you by any qualified professional.

Dr Patrizia Collard asserts the moral right to be identified as the author of this work.

ISBN: 978-1-59963-985-7

A CIP catalogue record for this book is available from the British Library.

10 9 8 7 6 5 4 3 2 1

Commissioning Editor Liz Dean
Senior Editor Leanne Bryan
Deputy Art Director Yasia Williams-Leedham
Designer Sally Bond
Picture Research Manager Jennifer Veall
Production Controller Allison Gonsalves

CONTENTS

HOW TO USE THIS BOOK

This book is packed with essential guidance and mindfulness techniques. Although it is not a religious practice, mindfulness helps us to "connect" with the self and others on a deep, immediate, and compassionate level. The kind of awareness that you can attain through mindfulness is that of an innocent being who fully experiences each moment as if it were unique. One way in which we can journey towards this state of mind is by choosing to slow down our lives, allowing ourselves to be human "beings" without constantly being "online" or doing: acting, striving, rushing.

Of course it would not be possible in one volume to cover the subject of mindfulness completely, and the struggles in life that it helps to alleviate. Therefore I have had to make decisions about which areas of mindfulness application I felt it was pertinent to include and which to leave out. I have endeavoured to make each chapter as independent as possible, so that you can read any one section in isolation, choosing whichever appeals to you first. You may wish to read the book from cover to cover, dip into it at your leisure, or simply open a page and see what offers itself up to you.

Part 1 introduces the origin and uses of mindfulness, followed by a discussion of the medical and therapeutic use of mindfulness interventions, including recent research on what mindfulness practice actually changes in our bodies and brains. It also explores the many different mindful therapies that are available, and looks at how mindfulness helps us to show compassion to ourselves and others.

Part 2 deals exclusively with the application of mindfulness in everyday

life: in family life, work, relationships, and so on. A large section of this part of the book describes the essential meditations that I recommend you to try (although I have omitted practices that are best taught by an instructor or guide). I have also included a sample eight-session course of MBCT (Mindfulness-Based Cognitive Therapy; see pages 65–70), because such courses are becoming increasingly popular. Finally, we look at how mindful living invites you to be aware, kind, compassionate, and all-inclusive for

Above: *Reconnecting with nature in a playful or adventurous way is one aspect of mindful living.*

the rest of your life: in your own daily life, in your personal, social, and work relationships, and as you age.

Interspersed with all this you will find a number of testimonies, stories, poems, and illustrations, for your inspiration and contemplation. You may like to buy a lovely notebook or diary in which to record the shifts in awareness that you experience as you follow the invitation to live mindfully that is offered within these pages.

PART 1

The origin and uses of mindfulness, including recent research

MINDFULNESS: ORIGINS & PIONEERS

Mindfulness was first brought to Western awareness in the 1960s, when Westerners travelled to the East in order to learn about meditation and yoga. The Beatles, Leonard Cohen, and other famous artists showed the public how much they had learned from Eastern philosophy and integrated it into their work, in turn inspiring Eastern gurus, yogis, and Zen teachers to come to the West to teach their insights.

Below: *The Beatles with Maharishi Mahesh Yogi. George Harrison was deeply touched by the message of peace as part of Transcendental Meditation and it had a profound effect on the rest of his life.*

Thich Nhat Hanh – the first mindfulness teacher in Europe

The origins of mindfulness date back to 2500 bce in the Sutras (a collection of aphorisms in Hindu or Buddhist philosophy), as well as being connected to Taoist, Sufi, and yogic philosophies.

The first text of importance to be translated into English in the 20th century was *The Miracle of Mindfulness* by the Vietnamese monk Thich Nhat Hanh (b. 1926). It was originally written as a letter from exile in France to one of his brothers, who had remained in Vietnam.

Nhat Hanh had founded the School of Youth for Social Services in Saigon. This grass-roots relief organization rebuilt bombed villages, set up schools, established medical centres, and resettled families left homeless during the Vietnam War. The centres that Nhat Hanh founded in the 1960s were intended to help those who had lost everything; to teach children; and to set up medical stations for both sides engaged in the conflict. The letter's intention was to support his brothers back home to continue their work in the spirit of love and understanding. Nhat Hanh wished simply to remind them of the essential discipline of mindfulness, even in the midst of very difficult circumstances.

When he was writing the letter in Paris there were several supporters from different countries attending the Vietnamese Buddhist Peace Delegation. So it was quite natural to think of people in other countries who might also benefit from reading his letter. Nhat Hanh suggested that the translator (an American volunteer) should translate it slowly and steadily – just two pages a day – and be aware of the feel of the pen and paper, of the position of his body, and of his breath, in order to maintain the essence of

---

Thich Nhat Hanh has written more than a hundred books and travels frequently to spread his message of peace.

---

mindfulness while doing this task. When the translation was complete, a hundred copies were printed on a tiny offset machine squeezed into the delegation's bathroom. Since then the little book has travelled far.

It has been translated into several other languages and distributed on every continent in the world. Prisoners, refugees, healthcare workers, psychotherapists, educators, and artists are among those whose life and work have been touched by *The Miracle of Mindfulness*. Denied permission to return to Vietnam, Thich Nhat Hanh now spends most of the year living in Plum Village, a community that he helped to found in France. It is open to visitors from around the world who wish to spend a mindfulness retreat there. The proceeds from the fruit of hundreds of plum trees are used to assist hungry children in Vietnam. Thich Nhat Hanh has written more than a hundred books and travels frequently to spread his message of peace.

Above: *The Vietnamese Thich Nhat Hanh, who decided at the age of ten to become a monk.*

Jon Kabat-Zinn – mindfulness pioneer in medicine

Jon Kabat-Zinn (b. 1944) has been a great influence on spreading mindfulness within the medical and psychological fields of the Western world over the last 33 years.

Zinn, who trained as a molecular biologist, became interested in Buddhism and studied Zen and Vipassana meditation for some time, and was inspired to bring meditation from its Buddhist origins into a more secular setting. In 1979 he gave up his promising scientific career and started a stress-reduction clinic at Massachusetts University Hospital.

The success of this programme, and the positive impact it had on the participants, was huge. Since then a lot of different mindfulness-based therapeutic schools have evolved and have changed the lives of many participants for the better. Even patients suffering from recurrent depression and other such ailments have a chance to get better – and stay better. Zinn therefore began to use mindfulness techniques to treat patients with chronic pain and other ongoing conditions. Due to the successful outcome of the initial patient groups treated with this approach, he started to develop his now world-famous MBSR (Mindfulness-Based Stress Reduction, see pages 75–6) programme, an eight-week course designed to introduce participants to mindfulness and coping with stress and chronic pain more effectively. In 1991 Zinn's book describing stress-reduction clinic's programme in Massachusetts, *Full Catastrophe Living*, was published and sold more than half a million copies across the world.

Eventually, at the World Congress of Cognitive Therapy held at Oxford in 1989, British psychologists and psychotherapists searching for new treatment models to combat recurring depression were introduced to mindfulness approaches and started to apply them. A book entitled *Mindfulness-Based Cognitive Therapy for Depression* was the result of their studies and was published in 2002. This forms the foundation of teaching MBCT for depression; it includes deep research, as well as humanity and kindness, and saw its second edition in 2013. The use of mindfulness for psychological and physical ailments continues to expand.

Below: *Dr Jon Kabat-Zinn who created MBSR, the first secular mindfulness course to help people learn to live with chronic pain and other diseases.*

Other important figures in modern mindfulness

In the 1940s, long before Jon Kabat-Zinn, psychologists and doctors like Wilhelm Reich used aspects of mindfulness psychology in their work. Reich had a profound influence on Fritz Perls, who developed Gestalt therapy (a kind of psycotherapy that focuses on individual freedom and responsibility).

erls was taught by Zen masters in the 1960s while staying in a Zen monastery in Japan, and he referred to mindfulness as "awareness practice". Many psychotherapists of the 1960s and 1970s were deeply influenced by bare attention – or mindfulness – which affected their life and work. The teachings of Thich Nhat Hahn and of the monk and teacher Nyanaponika Thera also left an impact on Ron Kurtz, who chose aspects of mindfulness in a very intentional and ordered way in the Hakomi process of Body-Centred

Psychotherapy in the 1970s. Kurtz and others founded the Hakomi Institute, where they practised this form of therapy. Their prime influences and ideas were based on mindfulness, non-violence, body–mind holism, and so on.

Right: *The work of Austrian psychoanalyst Wilhelm Reich helped shape the Gestalt therapy of Fritz Perls.*

The Buddha's influence on mindfulness

Siddhartha Gautama, who was later called the Buddha ("the Awakened One"), was born a prince in what is now Nepal 2,500 years ago, and it was predicted by a wise man that he would become a great religious leader.

His father, however, wanted him to become the next king and thus never allowed Siddhartha to leave the palace and see what life outside was like. The prince never questioned his father's decision, and got married and became the father of a son himself. But Siddhartha was always curious about life outside, and one day he visited a town and was deeply touched by the poverty, sickness and death he witnessed. He had never seen "suffering" to such an extent. This drove him to run away and embark on a spiritual journey that lasted about 14 years. He studied with famous spiritual teachers and learned to meditate and turn away from all the joys of life, although he realized, after years of living as an ascetic, that completely renouncing all pleasure was as unhelpful as living in splendour – as he had during his early life.

> If you enjoy something in the moment, but understand that it will not last forever, you will greatly reduce your suffering.

One day he chose to sit under the tree of wisdom and decided not to get up until he had the answer to how one could reduce suffering. After more than a week of meditation he

became enlightened. He realized that extreme emotions, such as complete attachment or rejection, caused suffering. If you enjoy something in the moment, but understand that it will not last forever, you will greatly reduce your suffering; similarly, if you can accept that there is suffering now but that it will pass, you will also suffer less. The Buddha refined his teachings and spread

Above: *The Lord Buddha portrayed as receiving a piece of bamboo containing water from an elephant and a beautiful fruit from a white monkey.*

them, and Buddhists developed them into meditation practices and monastic living practices.

One of the most important concepts of Buddhist philosophy is to accept that one's life experience frequently involves suffering, but that

there are refined and tested ways of alleviating this. The Buddha, however, always encouraged his students to test his teachings, to see whether they would actually help their own individual existence when put into practice. He warned his followers repeatedly of the dangers of dogma;

Above: *The term "mindfulness" comes from the Pali word sati. It is an essential part of Buddhist practice.*

for Buddha, his teachings were a way of life, a philosophy, and definitely not a religion. In the same way mindfulness is a practical way of leading your life, which is meant to be of benefit to you and others.

Taoism's influence on mindfulness

Another Eastern philosophy closely linked to, and therefore informing, mindfulness is Taoism. It offers an approach to life that is similar to mindfulness.

The term "Tao" (pronounced "dow", like "cow") refers to all that is – all of creation; it is life, both inside and around us. Taoism is about listening to your intuition as your main source of wisdom, rather than being led by convention and rules imposed from outside. Being in the moment, here and now, is equally important in Taoism. Living from moment to moment, you are liberated from the heavy load of worldly expectations. Unwanted and often unnecessary thoughts and worries in your mind are released, and this makes room for helpful and compassionate actions.

Another important aspect of Taoism is the letting go of all inner attachments. This does not mean that one should live one's life detached from other humans, or without relationships. Rather, it means that true security and freedom can only be found in the inner authority – the Tao – rather

Right: *Philosopher and poet Lao Tzu is said to be the author of the Tao Te Ching and the founder of Taoism.*

than in institutions that are enforced on the individual from outside. Such institutions and rules all too often come with restrictions and regulations, which then stand in opposition to one's personal inner authority.

Above: *"The flow" of nature simply occurs and creates and nourishes moment by moment.*

This way of life is closely related to mindfulness, as it requires an inner freedom and the ability to observe without judgement. Observing should even, if possible, come without naming what is being observed, as speech and thoughts already lead to a particular direction, reducing freedom of perception. Just as in many mindfulness meditations, living the Tao offers us the possibility to practise observing processes within ourselves. By doing so, we can develop a true understanding of the state in which we find ourselves at any given moment. Feelings are accepted, rather than restricted or held back. They are free to come and go.

Why mindfulness is important now

A new threat facing us in the 21st century is something we thought would make our lives easier: everyday technology.

A growing body of research on the subject of "burn-out" shows that more and more people use their smartphones and tablets in bed, while having a shower, and in other previously private and technology-free environments.

We constantly receive emails and text messages, and often we feel that unless we respond more or

---

People seem to have lost the ability to "simply be" and "enjoy the moment".

---

less immediately, people will think something dreadful must have happened to us; or that we might lose our job. Some individuals get so hooked that they can no longer find the "off" switch, and this can lead to burn-out or stress-related depression. Individuals who have got to this point may need as much as eight weeks of in-house treatment in a mental-health institution to recover, and will be required to change their lifestyle to prevent something even worse (such as a major physiological disease) from occurring. People seem to have lost the ability to "simply be", "enjoy the moment", and just have a cup of tea or eat lunch without continuing to work on their computer.

For many people, their involvement in sitcoms and reality shows is more intense than their real-life relationships. In Japan, for example, men have

fewer and fewer intimate relationships, finding emotional satisfaction with virtual girlfriends on their iPhones. A survey by Japan's Ministry of Health in 2010 found that 36 per cent of Japanese males aged 16–19 had no interest in sex – a figure that had doubled in the space of two years. Girlfriends can be found and dated in a Nintendo video game called *LovePlus* instead.

People seem to be trying to multitask and work in autopilot mode, but nobody actually benefits from this. The result of this lifestyle is a lack of peace and enjoyment, and a number of destructive emotions that lead to psychosomatic diseases. However, mindfulness is increasingly seen as a way of alleviating problems caused by overusing handheld technology.

Following the pioneering work of Jon Kabat-Zinn (see pages 13–14), psychotherapists in Canada and

Left: *Buzz-buzz-buzz – busy-busy-busy ... the frenetic energy of modern living can easily lead to burn-out.*

the UK began to understand that mindfulness interventions might be useful for reducing and improving psycho-logical disorders. The first best-seller in the realm of therapy books, Kabat-Zinn's *Mindfulness-Based Cognitive Therapy for Depression* showed how ancient wisdom was interwoven with Cognitive Therapy (which was founded by Aaron Becks in the 1960s and focuses on living in the here and now), in order to help patients in danger of relapsing into another depressive episode.

By reconnecting to the simple moments in life ... your focus of awareness will change.

When learning about mindfulness, it is important to realize that this skill may not necessarily "heal" you in a physical, tangible way. What it *will* do is change your perspective on your discomfort, and open up new possibilities for moving on from simply

REST + PAIN

MEDITATION + PAIN

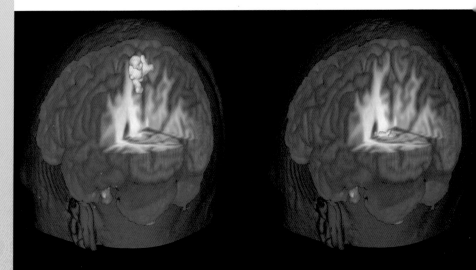

existing and struggling, to adventurous living. Should you be suffering from a long-term condition, such as chronic pain, with mindfulness you can learn to live with and around the pain, rather than focusing on it all the time. By reconnecting to the simple moments in life – by truly living moment by moment,

Above: *Experiments at the Wake Forest Baptist Medical Center in North Carolina show that, during meditation, a subject feels less pain than when at rest.*

rather than merely existing – your focus of awareness will change. The pain in *your* heel, for instance, will become a pain in *the* heel, and may even retreat into the background of your awareness.

RUMI'S TWO WORLDS

Look at the poem below, by the 13th-century Persian poet Rumi. Read it, then ask yourself which words or lines speak to you and in what way.

The Window

For years, copying other people,
   I tried to know myself.
From within, I couldn't decide
   what to do.
Unable to see, I heard my
   name being called.

Then I walked outside.
The breeze at dawn has secrets
   to tell you.
Don't go back to sleep.
You must ask for what you
   really want.
Don't go back to sleep.
People are going back and forth
   across the doorsill
Where the two worlds touch.
The door is round and open.
Don't go back to sleep.

RUMI (TRANSLATED BY COLEMAN BARKS)

MINDFULNESS: ORIGINS & PIONEERS

The first line of Rumi's poem, "For years, copying other people, I tried to know myself", shows the human dilemma: wishing to belong and be accepted. We try to be like those who raise us, as we believe them to be our role models. How often do we find out that, alas, this is not so? Only when we dare to look outside our "pack" – and other "limitations" that are forced on us by our cultures, laws, rules, and habits – can we see our true selves. We need to wake up from our "matrix", which holds us down and keeps us small, and free ourselves from interference, so that we can knowingly choose what is really right, and determine that we will no longer follow a path that is destructive to others and only serves a few, who think of themselves as important. When we move through the "round door" of love and compassion, we can no longer go back to sleep and simply watch how others are exploited or tormented.

One of the ways forward through this door may be to be kind to everyone – including, and indeed starting with, yourself; another answer might be to free yourself from "angst"; finally, you may choose to truly connect with what life offers you "here and now" and train your "muscle of awareness" to keep you in the present moment (rather than wandering back to the past, or forward towards a hypothetical future). It is only in this "now" that you can make a difference and experience life to the full.

Mindfulness is more than just meditation and awareness. It is a lifestyle, through the practice of which you can maintain a mindset of openness, childlike curiosity, adventure, and patience. It can help you move towards a gentler and kinder way of being. You can discover and work on these attitudes by practising mindfulness meditation.

Left: *When we connect to "this moment" the smallest little creature is perceived as the miracle it is.*

THE AWAKENING MIND: THE SCIENCE OF MINDFULNESS

We are all aware of the great importance of eating a wholesome, balanced diet and of exercising to keep our brains and bodies healthy. Understanding the benefits of regular mindfulness practice – for both mental and physical health – is also gaining momentum now. In the past it was thought that the adult human brain was "physiologically static" and that we were gradually losing nerve cells over time. Thankfully, scientists discovered the brain to be more pliable than we thought, and the term "neuroplasticity" came into use, describing how the brain can change over time, both at a cellular level and in entire brain regions.

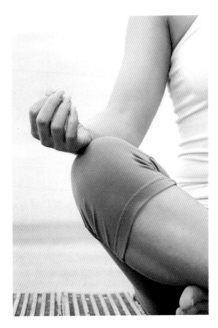

Left: *The benefits of regular mindfulness practice – including mindful meditation – are only now beginning to be recognized.*

BASELINE **MEDITATING**

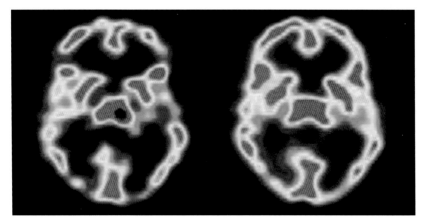

Mindfulness and the brain

Mindfulness has long been used as a tool to reduce stress, and it is known that the stress hormone cortisol is very damaging (toxic) to the brain.

With the introduction of sophisticated functional Magnetic Resonance Imaging (fMRI), scientists are increasing our understanding of how regular mindfulness practice produces positive changes in both brain activity and structure. Studies have shown positive changes in brain activity after just eight weeks of daily mindfulness

Above: *Scans of the brain of Dr Michael Baime from the Penn Program for Mindfulness show how mindfulness practice produces positive changes in brain activity and structure. The meditating brain is less activated and appears calmer than the other.*

practice (of approximately 30 minutes per day), leading to increased activity in brain regions associated with the regulation of emotions and with resilience to difficult and stressful life events. Changes in brain structure have also been demonstrated, with reduced activity in very primitive areas of the brain involved in our response to threat. There is also interest in mindfulness for managing pain; and research looking at brain images of people with pain has indicated a reduction of suffering associated with it.

While the human brain is remarkable in what it has enabled us to do as a species, it also has significant shortcomings that cause suffering at many levels.

Another interesting area of study is the reduction of cognitive function that is associated with ageing. As people live longer and dementia becomes more common, the possibility of mindfulness as a preventative tool for this debilitating condition is exciting. This is logical, considering the destructive effect of cortisol on the brain, and mindfulness as a way of reducing the production of this stress hormone in the body.

"Old brain" versus "new brain"

The complexity of the human brain has fascinated and puzzled scientists for many decades and there is still much that we struggle to understand. The question is often posed whether something so complex is capable of understanding itself. While the human brain is remarkable in what it has enabled us to do as a species, it also has significant shortcomings that cause suffering at many levels. This is partly explained by evolutionary limitations, as described by Professor Paul Gilbert from the University of Derby. Professor Gilbert separates the "old brain" psychology –

which developed approximately 120 million years ago – from "new brain" functions of around two million years, including complex thinking. Difficulties arise due to a conflict between "old brain" and "new brain" functions. Gilbert says that Mother Nature made sure we could survive, but did not much care for us having a "good time" while doing so. So we are able to recognize danger, and we also have the capacity to imagine it and relieve it.

Above: *By using mindfulness we can avoid angry "blow-ups" and respond to situations more effectively.*

Mindfulness helps us to notice when these "old brain" patterns are dominating, and we can then choose to bring wiser "new brain" activity to the fore. When we are angry, for example, we are unable to think clearly and are quite likely to react in habitual and unhelpful ways. However, by using mindfulness, we can restore our focus and learn to respond to situations more effectively, therefore avoiding adding to stressful situations.

Encouraging emotions to flow freely

Understanding of the human brain has also been advanced by the work of psychologists and Buddhist practitioners over thousands of years. Increasingly, Western scientists are working closely with Eastern meditation practitioners to share ideas

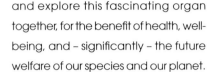

and explore this fascinating organ together, for the benefit of health, well-being, and – significantly – the future welfare of our species and our planet.

Buddhist philosophy describes the importance of free-flowing emotions for optimal mental health. However, many of us naturally protect ourselves from difficult emotions, such as anxiety or anger, by avoiding them. For some people this means working hard; for others, losing themselves in endless hours of television viewing, often compounding the problem when they view negative situations on the screen. When we shut out negative emotions, we also suppress positive emotions, and so we do not enjoy life as fully as we could. Many people learning to practise mindfulness report that they become more able to "live life to the full". With mindfulness we have a tool to cope with difficulty, approaching it with a kind and curious attention,

Left: *According to Buddhist philosophy, free-flowing emotions are essential for optimum mental health.*

Above: *Going on retreat gives us an opportunity to "feel" difficult emotions, and to be ourselves.*

rather than avoiding it. By allowing ourselves to feel difficult emotions, we find that they lessen in strength the next time they arise. Positive emotions are then free to "come up", and people report experiencing more joy.

The process described above intensifies during retreats. A retreat takes us away from these distractions and provides us with space to be with ourselves. Initially difficult emotions will inevitably arise, and healing tears often follow. However, towards the later stages of a retreat there is often laughter and a strong connection with others. One lady who attended a Buddhist retreat, during which the diet was vegan, commented, "I have never had such a good time on a glass of water and a lettuce leaf!"

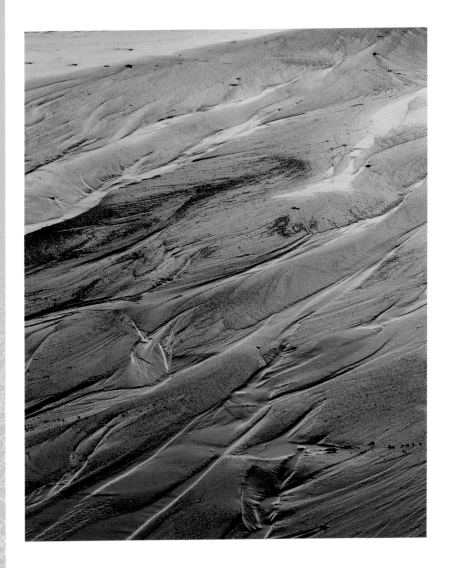

"Neurons that fire together, wire together"

First-person introspection, as utilized during Buddhist meditation, provides an important source of understanding our minds, and mindfulness helps us to do this. We learn to see more clearly the effects of thinking about our emotions and about the connection between our bodies and our minds. It is known that "neurons that fire together, wire together". If we are mindless, then we risk continuing to strengthen negative pathways in the brain. With mindfulness, we can deliberately choose to strengthen positive pathways, rewiring and changing our brains for the better. This understanding frees us to make better decisions for our well-being, benefiting those around us. We notice when the seductive pull of the "new brain" tendencies towards

Left: *By regularly practising mindfulness we can carve out positive pathways in the brain, in the same way that rivulets of water carve grooves into sand.*

"doing" begin to dominate, and relearn to connect with our senses and just "be". We revert back to "human beings" from "human doings".

A close friend who teaches mindfulness says, "As a health professional, for me to find time to practise every day, I needed to see good evidence that doing so would benefit me. I was inspired by the work of Richard Davidson and colleagues, and later by the work of (Sara) Lazar and colleagues (both in the area of neuroscience). Participants of my courses will be aware of my excitement when Lazar's group demonstrated that just 27 minutes of mindfulness practice per day for eight weeks reduced the grey-matter density of the amygdala. This brain region is such a primitive structure . . . that it had previously been thought impossible to evoke changes there. And yet here was a study demonstrating changes in this structure after only eight weeks."

CHANGES TO OUR BRAIN STRUCTURE

A few research findings in short, for those readers who like to check out facts:

- An eight-week course in MBSR (see pages 75–6) has been shown to reduce the amygdala's grey-matter density. Participants practised for 27 minutes per day on average.[1]

- Cortisol (the stress hormone) stimulates the amygdala, the gland that processes fear (see page 45), and oxytocin (the compassion hormone) "dampens amygdala arousal".[2]

- A Buddhist monk of French origin, Matthieu Ricard (pictured left), decided to live in Nepal after finishing his PhD in molecular biology in Paris. His amygdala has shrunk from the size of an almond to that of a raisin (see page 62) and he is said to be possibly the happiest man on the planet.[3]

- Mindfulness practice is seen as the "golden bridge" to the left pre-frontal cortex (see page 43).[4]

- Meditation experience is associated with increased cortical thickness.[5] A thicker cortex generally leads to a better ability to memorize.

fMRI and new pastures for humanity

Since the year 2000 studies in mindfulness, empathy, and compassion have grown exponentially and we are experiencing a shift in consciousness.

The wars on our planet that are ongoing – be they literally fighting for land or for financial power – have emphasized how egotistical and separated ways of living do not work any more. They cause levels of destruction that might sooner or later bring about the demise of the human race, or even of the whole planet. The cold way of living by principles based purely on the "theory of mind" now needs to be replaced by the "way of the heart", with its emphatic roots.

There are ways that can increase "thinking pathways" that could be described as empathic and compassionate. We are now in the privileged position of being able to see the workings of the brain in detail, using fMRI scanners. This shows us what we have known for a long time: that the brain is plastic – which means it can change. With the right methods, it can change to become better on many levels: less angry and frightened, more curious and generous, and more intelligent and creative.

"Mindfulness" as a buzzword

Mindfulness has recently been in the news a great deal: it has appeared on the cover of *Time* magazine, the *Guardian*, the *Daily Mail* (three days in a row), and even in the *Financial Times*. The journalist and *Guardian* columnist Madeleine Bunting argues that mindfulness is possibly the "most important life skill to learn" – ever. She explains that in a decade or so it will be recognized "as vital for the complexities of our information-rich lives". People from all walks of life now want to be trained in mindfulness, and I am presently running courses entitled "Keeping people at work", having been hired to do so by one of the best-known mental-health agencies in the UK. To top it all, an

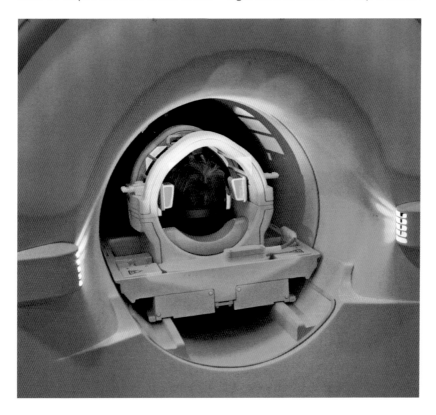

"All-Party Parliamentary Mindfulness Group" was launched on 7 May 2014, to look at how mindfulness can be rolled out most effectively in society. It wants to study the role that mindfulness could play in schools, in treating mentally ill adolescents, in the NHS, and in the workplace. Many people see mindfulness as a cheap, effective, and practical intervention for stress-filled lives, as well as a skill that can prevent people from breaking down, burning out, or becoming sick. The meeting was chaired by the MP Chris Ruane, who is the dynamic power behind the subject of mindfulness within the Houses of Parliament. He shared the information that 85 Members of Parliament had taken part in a mindfulness course (arranged by the Oxford Centre for Mindfulness), and there were about 20 Members from the House of Commons and House of Lords present at the meeting. Ruane explained

Left: *An fMRI scanner measures the activity of the brain by detecting changes in the flow of blood.*

that he and his fellow politicians had personally experienced the benefits of mindfulness, although the aim of the group was to enquire into how mindfulness can become part of life in the UK.

People from all walks of life now want to be trained in mindfulness.

The panel was made up of field experts, who provided compelling arguments and research results on the benefits of mindfulness, with powerful examples – such as working with violent offenders, who had been able to control their explosive actions due to the mindfulness training they had received. One expert also discussed how mindfulness can be effective in improving worker well-being, through the introduction of smarter systems within workplace institutions.

Tens of thousands of research papers have now been published,

THE AWAKENING MIND: THE SCIENCE OF MINDFULNESS

THE AWAKENING MIND: THE SCIENCE OF MINDFULNESS

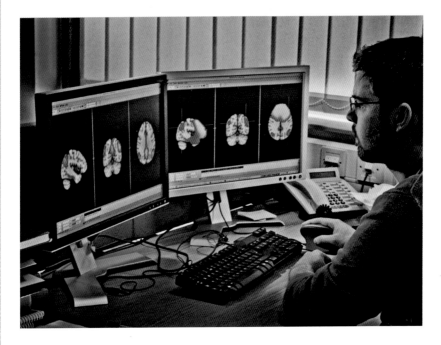

Above: *A researcher analyzes brain images that have been produced using an fMRI scanner.*

and mindfulness is used in fields as widespread as parent training, teaching in schools, in the criminal justice system, and in relapse prevention for a number of mental-health diagnoses, ranging from depression, anxiety, and anger disorders to the treatment of trauma.

Mindfulness also serves in the treatment of severe physical health issues, such as chronic pain, psoriasis, and certain forms of cancer. It improves the body's immune response, which has positive outcomes for those suffering from HIV, ME, chronic fatigue syndrome, MS, eating disorders and other addictions; and the list goes on!

How the brain works

Like the rest of the body, the brain consists of billions of cells. Brain cells, or neurons, are specially designed to transmit information to different regions of the brain as accurately and quickly as possible, covering the distance from one brain centre to another within milliseconds.

A typical neuron looks a bit like a tree. The information enters the cell via the branches (dendrites), is passed with the nucleus down the trunk (axon) to the roots (synapses) where it is transferred to the connecting branches of the next cell. So the brain can be seen as huge woodland (with approximately 100 billion cells) where information is passed between the trees, and, as in a wood, the more often you take a particular route, the broader and stronger it becomes. Therefore the more often we use a particular pathway in our brain (for instance, training a limb to do a certain movement, learning new words,

practising meditation, and so on), the broader and deeper-engrained this particular neural pathway becomes.

It is important to note that the brain is organized and structured in a particular way. Different parts of the brain are specialized in fulfilling particular tasks and can be seen as being connected to particular experiences. Furthermore, the brain can be seen as consisting of three major areas: the hindbrain, the midbrain and the frontal brain. The **hindbrain** (reptilian brain) is the "oldest" part of the brain. It evolved 500 million years ago and is responsible for automatic reflexes, breathing, heartbeat, coordination of moment, and sense perception. The **midbrain** (mammalian brain) is important for temperature control and the fine-tuning of movement, and plays an important role in the limbic system, which is thought to be vital for perception and the expression of emotions. The **frontal brain** (the "youngest" part) consists of two hemispheres, which are particularly developed in humans: the thalamus and the hypothalamus. Because there are so many neurons in it, the human brain had to be "folded",

giving it the shape and appearance we know today. The forebrain, or **cortex**, is responsible for controlling cognitive, sensory, and motor functions, as well as regulating eating, sleeping, reproductive functions, and the display of emotions.

The cortex can be divided into four lobes: the frontal, temporal, parietal, and occipital lobes. Again, each of these has a particular responsibility.

Below: *The neurons in our brains are responsible for transmitting information quickly and accurately.*

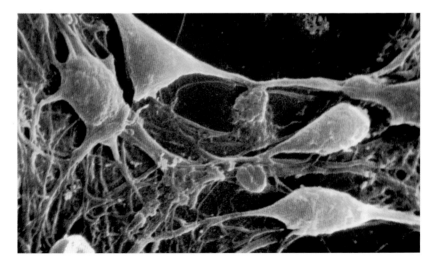

Cognitive skills are associated with the **frontal lobe**; those skills include reasoning, attention, comprehension of speech, the expression of emotions, empathy, short-term memory, and problem-solving, among others. In the very front of the brain the so-called **pre-frontal cortex** is vital for complex thoughts, and represents our attention-association area; it is connected to the visual parts of the brain and is therefore involved in generating images as thoughts and daydreams, which appear spontaneously and randomly in a relaxed mind. In an occupied or focused mind some images are more important than others and get more attention. So the frontal cortex screens incoming information for relevant thoughts and images, which is particularly important when meditating. The middle part of the pre-frontal cortex is said to be particularly important for processes like the balance between activity and relaxation; inner balance and the regulation of emotions; the flexibility to be able to respond freely to a given situation and not be forced to react immediately; empathy due to perception of inner processes; the modulation of anxiety via the inhibition of deeper structures (the amygdala); and so on. Many of those important processes respond to and improve through the practice of mindfulness.

The **parietal lobe** is especially relevant for sensory perception, language, and selective attention. If damaged, patients suffer from a distorted perceptual awareness (there is a famous case discussed in the fascinating book by Oliver Sachs, *The Man Who Mistook His Wife for a Hat*).

The visual-association area, long-term memory, the detection and recognition of sounds, and the sensory aspects of speech are associated with the **temporal lobe**, which also includes two structures belonging to the limbic system: the hippocampus

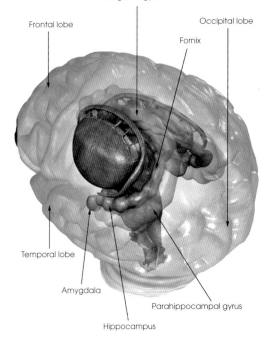

Cingulate gyrus

Frontal lobe

Occipital lobe

Fornix

Temporal lobe

Amygdala

Parahippocampal gyrus

Hippocampus

Above: *An anatomical illustration of the human brain displaying this vital organ in all its complexity*

and the amygdala. These two areas are of special interest because they are thought to be involved in generating emotional behaviour, as well as long-term memory. Because of the connection between the limbic system and the visual-association area, it is possible that emotions can be directed towards certain objects, as well as the objects being able to trigger a specific emotional response. The **hippocampus** is especially important for the formation of memory; most of our emotionally charged memories are stored here. Input from our senses is assigned with emotional value in the hippocampus, explaining why remembering an extremely negative or positive experience can still "feel" fresh and unchanged, even after years have passed. The term **amygdala** comes from the Greek word for almond, referring to the structure's shape. It plays a vital part in the expression of emotions such as fear, rage, and love, due to its intense connections with different parts of the brain, such as the pre-frontal cortex and the hippocampus. When activated, the amygdala triggers violent, fearful, or aggressive behaviour. People who suffer from a dysfunctional amygdala become incapable of any type of emotional expression.

Finally, the **occipital lobe** is responsible for processing visual information, including visual recognition. If it is damaged, we lose the ability to see, even though our eyes may work perfectly well. The brain can no longer process the incoming information – a condition that is known as "cortical blindness".

How physiology affects mood

The all-important passing on of information between the neurons in your brain works through impulses (within the cell) and through chemical **neurotransmitters**. Neurotransmitters such as serotonin, dopamine, and noradrenaline act as "messengers", delivering the information from one cell to another. They are stored and released by the cell into the "branches" of the next cell, where they are picked up by its receptors. There the message is transformed back into an electrical impulse.

To deliver a message correctly this system has to be perfectly balanced. The right neurotransmitters have to be available for the right amount of time in the right combination. If this balance cannot be maintained, it affects a person's mood. There is, for example, a significant correlation between lack of serotonin and depression, and that is why many antidepressants focus on inhibiting serotonin from being used up too quickly. It is not yet known whether the lack of the neurotransmitter causes diseases like depression, or whether the depression is there first and causes decreasing amounts of certain neurotransmitters. What we do know is that certain activities can trigger the release of neurotransmitters, which can then have an impact on our mood.

Oxytocin – the compassion hormone

We not only respond to fear (as seen in our "fight or flight" response mechanism), but also to compassion. Our heart rate goes down and we experience a sense of soothing and calm. The hormone named oxytocin was originally known to stimulate labour and help milk-flow in lactating women; it also helps the new mother to bond with her baby, become a better mother, and in general preserve closer relationships with others. Interestingly,

but not surprisingly, it is also released when making love and reaching a climax, and the "special feeling and elevated mood" can last for minutes or even hours. Our relationship with and love for our partner will deepen, the more oxytocin is released.

We not only respond to fear, but also to compassion. Our heart rate goes down and we experience a sense of soothing and calm.

Oxytocin increases when we are moved by compassion (just as it is when we are being touched, or when we eat chocolate). It suppresses the activity of the amygdala, the gland that processes fear and communicates it to the rest of the brain. Oxytocin also increases different kinds of human interaction and actions: it stimulates us to lean forward, smile, and use peaceful hand gestures. This chemical reaction increases the more we act

upon it: so more compassion, and feeling better, triggers us to act even more compassionately, and so on. Oxytocin can also be increased by stimulating our senses: by listening to calming sounds, scenting certain smells, experiencing sunlight and massage (touch).

Dr R Sahelian wrote a paper on oxytocin in which he showed that the hormone has even more health

Above: *A polarized light micrograph of crystals of oxytocin – the "compassion hormone".*

benefits than have already been mentioned. It can assist in decreasing blood pressure and cortisol levels; it can make us deal better with pain, stress, and fear; and it can speed up physical healing. The positive social interactions of daily life continuously activate this system. Certain types of psychotherapy and coaching are

able to stimulate it too, and MBCT is one form of such support.

Oxytocin is found not only in the brain, but also in other body parts, such as the kidneys, heart, pancreas, uterus, placenta, and testes.

Compassion's effect on the amygdala

Mindfulness meditation has a positive impact on well-being, as well as developing certain structures of the brain. In a recent study at the University of Wisconsin, researchers found that subjects in an fMRI scanner showed different responses in their amygdala (see page 45), depending on which instruction they received. Two groups were formed; both were shown a picture of someone suffering. The participants of one group were given a "compassion instruction": if they saw someone suffering, they should imagine thoughts and phrases

Left: *Examples of balance can be found everywhere, even in those places where you least expect them.*

The balance of activity and relaxation

Relaxation is essential for life, and knowledge about its importance can be found in all cultures and all centuries. As a general rule, relaxation can be achieved by:

- Everyday practices, such as sleeping, taking a shower or bath, playing, dancing, having a good conversation, praying, and so on.

- Substances that have an effect on the mind, such as alcohol, some herbal teas, illegal drugs, medication, and so on.

- Special techniques to induce relaxation intentionally, such as mindfulness.

such as "May you be well, may you be safe, may you be happy and free of suffering". They were instructed to develop and feel compassion for the person they were going to be presented with. Interestingly, these participants showed a significantly weaker response in their amygdala to the disturbing picture than the other group, who had not been given any instructions beforehand. So the amygdala responded less severely if compassion had been introduced into the equation.

Stress and relaxation

It is most important for the functioning of the body's system that there is a *balance* between periods of activation and periods of relaxation. Too much of either can lead to ill health, as it compromises the immune system. Some pressure can be helpful and motivating; stress, however, is always destructive. All beings need a certain amount of peace and quiet

and, scientifically speaking, relaxation has three major purposes:

- It brings the body's system back to "square one" – into a state from where new arousal and activity are possible (for concentration or movement, for example)

- It provides room for regeneration, after phases of prolonged arousal and activity

- It reduces hyperactivation of the sympathetic nervous system (see page 55).

Psychologists Robert M Yerkes and John D Dodson developed a theory concerning an inverted U-shaped correlation between performance and physiological and/or mental activation. This suggested that more activation (pressure, not stress) leads to a better performance – but only

Above: *Relax - simply be and let go of "doing".*

up to a certain point. When you enter the "stress point" and your chosen activities become too much for you to cope with, you end up hyper-aroused and your performance decreases. So putting yourself under pressure to achieve more can only lead to success within well-defined boundaries. To remain at the ideal level of arousal, awareness of "stress symptoms" really is paramount. The more mindful you are, the more you will be able to use meditation or relaxation as a regular means of staying "in the zone".

Stress is known to be a major risk factor in the origin and duration of disease. Therefore an effective means of relaxation is essential to maintain physical and psychological well-being. This is one of the wonderful side-effects that mindfulness can provide. Donald Meichenbaum, a world-renowned psychotherapist and stress educator, says, "Relaxation is the aspirin of stress reduction."

The connection between mind and body

One of the first psychologists to study the connections between physical and psychological processes in the human mind and body was Edmund Jacobson (1888–1983), who researched the topic in the 1920s at Harvard University.

What he found was most significant: that mental arousal also leads to an increase in the tension of muscles, which Jacobson could measure with an EMG (electromyogram), a device that he invented for this purpose. He found that in mental/emotional arousal, especially when fear is present, the muscles contract. He developed muscular relaxation (first tensing and then relaxing muscles on the out-breath), which led to a decrease of activation of the sympathetic nervous-system arousal (a decrease in "fight or flight" response), which was responsible for the physical signs of stress in the body.

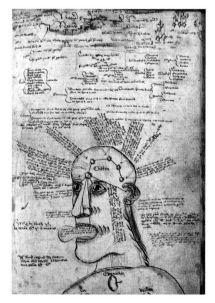

Above: *A page from Aristotle's* De Anima, *in which he observes that, "attempting to define the soul is one of the most difficult questions in the world".*

Jacobson could now prove what ancient cultures had known for decades; and what Aristotle, for example, had written about it in *De Anima*: that there is a highly significant connection (psychosomatic) between body and mind. Although we can think of those two systems as being independent, they are actually two sides of the same coin and cannot be separated.

If one part (say, the body) is agitated, then the other part (the mind) will follow. We are not stressed or agitated by occurrences themselves, but by whatever special significance we give them. For one person, a dog might be their best friend, might be connected with memories of a happy childhood, and this might evoke feelings of joy, even love. For another person, this same dog might trigger different thoughts and feelings such as fear and distress. This state of anxiety influences the way our bodies respond. In order to achieve a different physiological state, it makes sense to put the mind into a different mode, and this is exactly what mindfulness does. A relaxed mind will help the body to follow suit, and mindfulness can serve as a highly efficient relaxation technique, providing not only a pleasant effect (body sensations), but also contributing essentially to mental and physical health and well-being.

So how does the brain respond to intense stress? In reaction to a situation that you believe you cannot handle, part of the brain called the hypothalamic-pituitary-adrenal (HPA) system is activated. This system triggers the production and release of the primary stress hormone **cortisol**, which is very important in organizing systems throughout the body (including the heart, lungs, circulation, metabolism, immune systems, and skin) to deal quickly with a life-threatening situation.

However, cortisol also feeds back into the hypothalamus and

hippocampus in the brain. When those areas are hyperactivated over a long term – because your job is too demanding, for example, or your relationship is toxic – they become exhausted and thus less functional. The HPA system also releases chemical messengers such as dopamine and adrenaline, which activate the amygdala. And if the amygdala is hyperactivated, you may feel anxious all the time and eventually burn out.

While high levels of adrenaline float through your system, they suppress activity in areas at the front of the brain concerned with short-term memory, concentration, inhibition, and rational thought. They also interfere with the ability to handle difficult social or intellectual tasks and behaviours during that time. Have you noticed that stressed individuals are rarely empathetic, creative, or kind?

At the same time the hippocampus is storing the emotionally loaded experience as "long-term memory".

The effects of stress on the brain and body

Having discussed briefly how the brain works and how stress can affect us, it's time to look at the havoc that ongoing stress chemicals can cause in the brain and body. Below is a brief description:

Left: *When too much stress exhausts the system this can lead to breakdown and even burn-out.*

- We have two nervous systems: the parasympathetic and the sympathetic nervous systems.

- The **parasympathetic** state is the one we ideally want to be in as often as possible; it is the state in which we feel relaxed, at peace, in equilibrium. We only switch to the **sympathetic** nervous system (the SNS) when we feel threatened. So this latter state is switched on for survival, and thus needs to be swift and effective. Our forefathers survived attacks by wild predators because of this highly effective system.

- Nowadays, however, this system gets switched on many times each day and often remains switched on – if, for example, a particular project at work makes you feel out of your depth a lot of the time. Long-term SNS activation causes damage to almost all regions of the body and mind (chronic stress through hyperactivation of the SNS).

- This hyperactivation can create a number of physical abnormalities, such as autoimmune dysfunctions: lupus, multiple sclerosis, thyroid problems, chronic fatigue, frequent infections of the respiratory tract, the skin, and the digestive tract, to mention but a few.

- We are also aware that this hyper-arousal leads to psychological diseases, such as depression, suicidal thoughts, and burn-out – to point out just the tip of the iceberg.

In primitive times this brain action would have been essential for survival, since long-lasting memories of dangerous situations would be critical for avoiding similar threats in the future. So, if you get stuck in a lift once, you will remember this one experience, rather than the 2,000 times when the lift worked fine. This can lead to avoidant behaviour (phobias).

The stress response also affects the heart, lungs, and blood circulation. Breathing becomes rapid, and the lungs take in more oxygen. The spleen discharges red and white blood cells, allowing the blood to transport more oxygen throughout the body. Blood flow may actually increase by 300–400 per cent, strengthening the muscles, lungs, and brain for added demands. You can now run faster or hit harder.

The immune system changes when stress chemicals float through the body. The system now focuses more on areas that could get wounded in a fight. The immune-boosting troops are sent to the body's front lines, where injury or infection is most likely to occur, such as the skin and the lymph nodes. Other areas, however, are left unprotected. So long-term stress can be responsible for respiratory and other infections. Stress also shuts down digestive activity, a non-essential body function during short-term periods of hard physical work or crisis. This can lead to gastrointestinal problems, frequent urination, and even diarrhoea.

In a sense, you survive dangerous situations because of this very effective stress response. That's good, isn't it? If, however, the SNS is switched on more or less non-stop (because of crowded trains or roads, high demands, little time off, and so on), you will experience sickness. The most commonly reported ailments are: fatigue, lack of energy and motivation, sleep disorders (reduced slow-wave sleep, early or frequent wakening), appetite disruption, depletion, depression, immunodeficiency, frequent

Above: *The stress response increases blood flow in the body, meaning you can run faster and hit harder.*

illness/infections, thyroid/endocrine burn-out, obesity/diabetes, autoimmune disorders such as chronic fatigue, psoriasis, lupus, fibromyalgia, chronic pain, chemical sensitivity, high blood pressure, infertility, and so on, to name but a few.

The stress hormone cortisol is a toxic substance if it is in our system long-term. It impairs brain regions, suppresses secondary immunity, overactivates the amygdala (causing fear/negativity) and the adrenals (burn-out/weight-gain), decreases the growth of new brain cells (making us stick to old, fearful thinking), causes atrophy of the hippocampus (which can produce 30,000 new cells daily, but not if too-high levels of cortisol are present), and impairs hippocampal memory (spatial navigation, autobiographical memory – no memory or impaired memory, such as getting lost in areas that should be familiar to us). No new cell growth means no ability to form new associations/neural pathways (new ways of thinking). And impairment of the cingulate cortex (linking memory and emotion) and of the pre-frontal cortex (executive function, decision-making) means that new projects don't get done or lack the creative spark. Chronic stress therefore strengthens negative networks and weakens positive ones.

Mindfulness as a stimulant to changes in the brain

All this fantastic information has only been available to us for just over a decade, and fMRI scanners can now see the working brain and show us how stress or meditation affects this vital organ.

> The more we practise mindfulness, the stronger and wider the new path to more freedom of choice and less stress will become.

A stressed brain cannot learn or retain new information. It will purely fight for its own survival and will lack mindful compassion towards others. Without necessarily being aware of it, we tend to perform in the same way (walk down the same path) when we are presented with a situation similar to the one in which the neuronal pathway was initially developed. This is why we often behave in the same way when we are in stressful, frightening, or emotional situations.

On the other hand, we can see a way out of this sometimes vicious circle by remembering this principle: the more we practise a certain behaviour/way of thinking, the easier it will be for us in the future to stick to it. So the more we practise mindfulness, the stronger and wider the new path to more freedom of choice and less stress will become.

So if the brain is in the correct relaxed state, new neuronal ways can be created that can transform our thinking and our actions. An analogy is to think of our brain as a lawn. To stimulate certain cells into a particular action can be seen as similar to walking over a lawn. When we walk over a lawn, our feet bend and tread down the grass and leave a small path; and in the brain our cells form new connections between each other, which in turn also form a kind of path. The more often we walk along this new path, and the more frequently we

Above: *The less we entertain old ways of thinking, the more overgrown old neuronal pathways will become.*

perform this action or task, the wider and more permanent the path on the lawn will become – and the more connections between neurons will be established. Eventually this will lead to new ways of thinking and behaving. Old neuronal pathways will eventually get "overgrown" and less and less used. They cannot be deleted, but they can become redundant.

As can be shown by various studies that have taken place in the last 20 years, mindfulness can lead to measurable changes in the brain. Not only do certain areas grow, but the patterns of activity responsible for depression or obsessive-compulsive behaviour change.

Mindfulness and emotional outcomes

Mindfulness is also an important factor in retaining a healthy self-esteem. Research shows that low self-esteem levels are connected to a number of psychological illnesses and diseases, such as depression and anxiety disorders.

A recent study by Jan Burg and Johannes Michalak at Ruhr-Universität Bochum in Germany has shown that there is a significant correlation between mindfulness and our level of self-esteem, as well as its stability. These findings also support the importance of mindfulness for the overall quality of physical and mental well-being. Ongoing practice of mindfulness meditation can reduce the size of the amygdala, which in turn leads to a reduced stress response.

Mindfulness-based approaches and the impact they can have on our well-being (as well as on the outcome of mental-health problems) have been scientifically tested on a broad scale. One project involved nearly 2,000 participants in just one meta-analysis (the common outcome and insights obtained from a number of different studies). Comparing five meta-analyses from recent years, it can be concluded that mindfulness-based approaches are sufficiently beneficial for general psychological health and stress management for people to include them in their daily life-routine, as well as for those who suffer from mental-health issues.

Since 2008, scientists from New York University have been examining the brains of meditating Buddhist monks using fMRI scanners, which show where most activity is taking place. The researchers suggest that the human brain is organized into two different networks, each active and responsible for dealing with different tasks, such as pouring a cup of tea (extrinsic network) or dealing with emotions (intrinsic, default network). It seems that the monks, when in a state of deep meditation, found a profound harmony between themselves and their surroundings, being able to keep both the extrinsic and intrinsic networks active at the same time. Researchers believe that this ability may lead to the feeling of harmony that people who meditate may experience.

The 68-year-old French monk Matthieu Ricard, who turned to Buddhism some 40 years ago, has been labelled by the popular media as "possibly the happiest man alive". He had been attending retreats in Nepal throughout his student years and, after finishing his PhD in molecular biology at the Pasteur Institute in Paris, decided to live in Nepal and become a monk. He is the Dalai Lama's French translator and has been extremely keen to observe scientific proof for meditation and well-being. He has been known to spend two hours or more in a scanner, performing several meditations while

Left: *The monk Matthieu Ricard has his brain scanned while meditating for the University of Wisconsin study.*

his brain is observed and analysed. Scientists at the University of Wisconsin have shown that M. Ricard's brain produces high levels of gamma-waves when practising "unlimited compassion meditation" towards all beings (gamma-waves are linked with consciousness, attention, learning, and memory). Perhaps even more surprising is the massive activity in M. Ricard's left pre-frontal cortex compared to the right pre-frontal cortex. Furthermore, his amygdala , which processes fear, has shrunk from the size of an almond to the size of a raisin. This all suggests that he has an overwhelmingly large capacity for happiness and joy, and is less likely to tend towards negativity.

Although research like this is still only in its infancy, remarkable results have been found in long-term practitioners, as well as in practitioners who did just 20 minutes of meditation a day during a three-week period. It can be concluded that meditation that focuses on compassion generates affection, empathy, and the desire to help, and thus changes the way the brain functions in an enduring way. Once upon a time humans were described as purely selfish and wanting to rule others, but today scientists are discovering that humans also possess

---

Meditation that focuses on compassion generates affection, empathy, and the desire to help, and thus changes the way the brain functions in an enduring way.

---

a deep-rooted ability to be good and kind. Immanuel Kant (1724–1804) is seen as one of the central figures in modern Western philosophy, and his opinion of compassion was blatantly negative when he wrote, "Such benevolence is called soft-heartedness and should not occur amongst human beings." Scientific investigation does, however, prove him wrong on many counts.

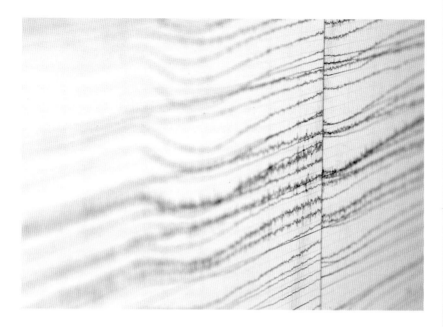

A study from Wisconsin University discovered that mothers who were viewing a photo of their little ones not only felt more compassionate, but their fMRI also showed that regions connected to a "general positive mood" lit up. Another study measured brain reactivity when subjects were asked to "help others". Again the pleasure centres showed activation.

Above: *Ricard's brain scans reveal how meditation can have positive long-term effects on brain function.*

This and many other studies prove that compassion is an inherent human reaction that is deeply rooted in our brains. However, our body also responds to others' vulnerability: whether we give or receive compassion, we feel relaxed, happy, and full of energy.

MINDFUL THERAPIES

After Jon Kabat-Zinn had created MBSR (see pages 75–6), other schools of psychological therapies followed suit and integrated aspects of mindfulness as a reliable tool into their programmes. MBSR was initially developed to help people cope better with chronic pain. More than ten years after its successful launch, Cognitive Behavioural Therapy (CBT) searched to find a way to prevent relapses into depression. Many different mindful therapies are now offered and are described on the pages that follow.

Below: *A group meets to share moment-to-moment experiences during a mindfulness training course.*

MBCT: Mindfulness-Based Cognitive Therapy

MBCT is a development of Cognitive Behavioural Therapy and has also been called part of the "third wave of CBT".

Cognitive Behavioural Therapy was first created by Aaron Beck in the 1960s in order to help depressed and suicidal patients. The "second wave of CBT" refers to the combining of cognitive and behavioural interventions. MBCT was initially devised to help those clients who responded well to CBT and yet repeatedly relapsed into another phase of depression. Nowadays, MBCT is used in many different areas, such as schools, mental health, physical health, relationship therapy, and addiction.

The concept

MBCT is based on an integration of CBT for depression, with components of mindfulness practice. MBCT has didactic elements, which give the participants information about the particular difficulty they are dealing with. In the case of depression, participants are given information on the universal characteristics of

---

MBCT is used in many different areas, such as schools, mental health, physical health, relationship therapy, and addiction.

---

depression to help them recognize their personal "relapse signatures" (such as wanting to withdraw from others, changing sleep and eating patterns, and so on). The mind pattern

MINDFUL THERAPIES

that makes people vulnerable to depressive relapse is known as "rumination", in which the mind repetitively reruns negative thoughts. The core skill that MBCT teaches is to deliberately "shift mental gears". There is little emphasis in MBCT (as there is in conventional CBT) on attempting to change unhelpful thoughts to more rational ones; rather, the focus is on *systematic* training to become more aware, moment by moment, of physical sensations and of thoughts and feelings as mental events. This facilitates a "de-centred" relationship to thoughts and feelings, in which

Below: *Become aware of life's miracles: wherever you go, they are there, waiting to be discovered.*

one can view them as aspects of experience that move through our awareness and are not necessarily the reality at any given moment. "We are not our thoughts!"; or "Thoughts are not facts!"

The mind pattern that makes people vulnerable to depressive relapse is known as "rumination".

The key themes of MBCT include experiential learning (Body Scan, pages 117–23; sitting meditation; mindful movement, pages 150–63) and the development of an accepting, open attitude with which one intentionally faces the problems one encounters. Increased mindfulness assists early detection of relapse-related patterns of negative thinking, feelings, and body sensations, enabling them to be addressed at a stage when this may be much easier than if such warning signs were not noticed or were even ignored.

MBCT has traditionally been used as a group intervention to teach recovered, recurrently depressed patients to disengage from negative thinking that may lead them to relapse into another episode. J D Teasdale (one of the founders of MBCT) found out that even a minor increase in sadness could reactivate "depressive thinking neuro-pathways" in formerly depressed client groups. CBT treatment had indeed been able to deactivate negative thinking, although it could not "delete" it from the "hard disk" of the mind. Each new episode of depression hard-wired these depressive thinking patterns more and more, and hence relapse tended to become activated more frequently and easily, the more depressive episodes had been experienced.

Research and development

MBCT is relatively cost- and time-effective and is now included in the

UK's National Institute of Clinical Excellence (NICE) guidelines for the prevention of recurrent depression. There is an increasing evidence base regarding the effectiveness of mindfulness-based approaches. I will point out here a few research publications of the many hundred that give evidence of the efficacy of MBCT – for example, the 2003 study by Rosenzweig, Reibel, Greeson and Brainard, which demonstrated the lowering of psychological anguish among medical students; in 2003 the R M McCraty study in the *Journal of Alternative and Complementary Medicine* demonstrated a reduction in blood pressure and an improvement in job satisfaction in employees with high blood pressure; the 2004 study undertaken by Richard Davidson highlighted the improved changes in brain and immune function brought about through mindfulness meditation; and the 2008 study by James Walsh and myself saw an improvement in the well-being of participants in all areas of their life.[6]

The Oxford Mindfulness Centre is a UK-based charity working with partners around the world to prevent depression and enhance human potential through the use of MBCT. It

Left: *When we are depressed, negative thoughts can become oppressive and cloud our thinking*

Right: *The black dog has long been used as a metaphor for depression; a dark, inescapable presence that follows you wherever you go.*

MINDFUL THERAPIES

supports an international centre of excellence within Oxford University for research into the effectiveness of mindfulness and the development of mindfulness programmes for therapy. MBCT has also been expanded to other treatment areas, as seen in the research into chronic fatigue by Christina Surawy, into eating disorders by Jill Roberts, and into patients who recurrently become suicidal as well as depressed by Mark Williams.

There is an increasing evidence base regarding the effectiveness of mindfulness-based approaches.

MBCT was developed as a prevention tool and was initially researched through a three-site randomized control trial (RCT) by Williams, Teasdale and Segal. In a multi-centre RCT conducted in Toronto, Cambridge and Bangor, 145 participants were allocated to receive either treatment as usual (TAU) or, in addition to TAU, eight classes of MBCT. All the participants in the study had no symptoms of depression for at least three months and were off antidepressant medication when they entered the trial. They were known to be vulnerable to future depression, though, because they had all had at least two episodes previously that met the criteria for major depression (the final episode having occurred within the previous two years). The sample was arranged on entry by the number of previous episodes (two only, or more than two). The participants were followed up for 12 months after the eight-week programme. The results showed that MBCT helped those who were the most severe cases, and substantially reduced the risk of relapse in those who had had three or more previous episodes of depression (reducing it from 66 to 37 per cent).

THE EFFECTS OF DEPRESSION
THE STORY OF JEANETTE WINTERSON

Anybody who has ever tried to explain the phenomenon of depression is inevitably referring to *their* depression. However, a certain mood and mind-state are often mentioned that call up the image of someone curling up in the back of a cave in darkness and waiting in limbo until something happens. And initially there seems to be no light at the end of the tunnel. One vivid and insightful description of depression was given by the writer Jeanette Winterson, who described in a documentary how she was totally unprepared for it.

Born in 1959 in Manchester, Jeanette was given up for adoption and was brought up by a fanatical Christian couple. She endured harsh punishments, including having the Old Testament read to her over and over again, and repeatedly being thrown out of the house and having to spend long, dark, freezing hours sitting on the front step of the house in which her adoptive family lived.

Nevertheless she was able to escape into her mind and tell herself stories to avoid going mad. In general she had the ability to win against the odds. She was thrown out by her adoptive mother at the age of 16, applied to Oxford University and graduated as one of the first working-class girls to read English literature. She coped with never being visited by remembering the stories that had helped her survive her childhood – they now served as material to enable her to write her own novels. She says about herself, "I always found the luminous part of life and great joy, even when it was tough."

In 2007, however, when a long-term relationship ended unexpectedly, she was suddenly thrown into the abyss of despair. Even enduring a brutal childhood, living in a car at the age of 16 for several months, and being without support at university had never managed to uproot her in such a devastating way.

Her depression felt to her like a physical blow to the stomach, chest, and knees. At this time of need, *language* (her "God") deserted her and left her in an abandoned place. She speaks about how difficult it is even to begin describing what she was going through then. Her mind was in agony; she would often curl up and wait for the pain to pass. It was a frightening experience, and she was mostly unable to share it with others, as she felt ashamed for having these negative emotions:

how could she possibly justify being so miserable? After all, she reasoned, she was a successful writer, had no financial worries, and had many wonderful friends.

However, during this time of darkness she could neither access her strength nor feel in touch with her positive, ever-curious, and adventurous self ("the space that was me"). More and more often she had the strong desire just to be gone, rather than carry on this "lukewarm existence". She felt she could not escape the "fire" (breakdown; depression). It was getting worse and she still refused to see a doctor, as she did not want to go on medication. She says that her "life before was gone forever". So she decided to end her life, but was saved by one of her cats meowing and rousing her from semi-consciousness. She explains that, at that moment, "I literally came to my senses ... and watched myriads of stars in the sky."

In this story we see how depression can drive one to lack the will to carry on living. MBCT endeavours to help one understand the signs of depression, and teaches that any moment might offer one the opportunity to start afresh.

Other therapeutic applications of mindfulness

There is currently a lot of general interest in mindfulness-based interventions, and research is focusing on a vast spectrum of disease management.

Teaching participants to become more mindful assists them in reconnecting to the experience of "being" rather than "doing". This, in turn, increases their individual effectiveness and, as a by-product, personal productivity.

In psychotherapeutic work "being mindful" is a life skill that expands alertness and helps us to be truly present, and it is taught in a variety of therapeutic approaches (aside from MBCT), described over the next few pages. MBSR, for example, is used generically, but in particular for chronic pain management and stress. MBCC (see pages 77–9), on the other hand, helps people deal with stress at work, among other things. ACT is another type of behaviour therapy that uses some aspects of mindfulness for overcoming low moods or anger. And DBT has helped adolescents with borderline personality disorders, who tend to use drugs and engage in self-harm.

Left: *Stress causes even simple everyday actions to become insurmountable obstacles.*

Mindfulness-Based Stress Reduction (MBSR)

MBSR is a group-based programme that was designed and developed by Jon Kabat-Zinn (see pages 13–14) and his colleagues at the University of Massachusetts Medical School Center for Mindfulness (CFM), for patients with an extensive variety of physical and mental-health problems.

Plenty of research has investigated the outcome of this eight-week course since late 1979. CFM has delivered MBSR to people needing medical help, and in 1993 Bill Moyers, a well-known American reporter,

participated in the programme and had one of the courses filmed. The series looked at a variety of alternative-medicine programmes

Below: *Participants taking part in MBSR programmes are trained intensively in mindfulness meditation.*

and was entitled *Healing from Within*. This was how MBSR became known to a much wider audience, and the series triggered huge interest in both the general and the medical population.

By the beginning of the new millennium more than 10,000 patients had completed the CFM course. It was then that Kabat-Zinn and other trainers started teaching MBSR in prisons, in rundown inner-city areas, in education, and among medical students and professional sport and corporate environments. MBSR is now

Above: *MBSR has been successfully taught in prisons.*

an acknowledged treatment option in the field of integrative medicine within behavioural medicine and general healthcare. Its potential lies not only in treatment, but also in the prevention of illness.

In MBSR the ancient tradition of Buddhist mindfulness is adapted from its use as a spiritual practice and is presented as an accessible, secular treatment option. It helps participants to conquer many difficulties that are faced when suffering from a variety of physical and psychological ailments. The original training is not modified for any particular diagnosis, and yet MBSR research has shown overall positive results for those suffering from chronic pain, fibromyalgia, multiple sclerosis, generalized anxiety disorder and panic attacks, psoriasis, certain types of cancer, and other ailments. Participants are trained intensively in mindfulness meditation and yoga movements, and embrace information on stress and life-skills.

Mindfulness-Based Cognitive Coaching (MBCC)

MBCC brings together two approaches in a model that provides the client with more control over, and enjoyment of, his or her daily life.

The synthesis between mindfulness training and cognitive behavioural coaching that led to the birth of MBCC provides the individual with skills and strategies to devise new and healthier beliefs about self, others, and the world in general, and with the ability to connect to the present. These skills are interwoven with awareness training – an example might be helping clients to identify self-defeating core beliefs that lead to unhelpful emotional and behavioural consequences.

Being mindful – that is, present in this moment when your life is actually happening – differs significantly from the way in which the 24/7 lifestyle has tended to shape people's experience in the 21st century. The ability to connect with what is termed

Above: *Mindfulness can help you see that thoughts are not facts – instead they are like "bubbles" in the mind – here one moment and gone the next.*

"the here and now" stimulates a completely different physiological response, as different parts of the nervous system become activated, allowing the experience to take on new meaning. There is significant evidence that learning to experience life from moment to moment can create calm and well-being, whereas over-planning, ruminating, and fretting trigger the so-called "stress response", which can lead to physical and mental illness.

MBCC tends to be applied to client groups who do not fall within the medical or therapeutic client arenas; it works with people who have begun to notice minor changes in their sleep, concentration,

Below: *Each moment that you practise mindfulness is a step in the right direction.*

and inter-personal relationships. The client is encouraged to consider how a more realistic and compassionate way of perceiving the world can increase personal effectiveness and decrease negative emotional outcomes for everyone concerned.

This process assists in the creation of the behavioural changes that are required to produce a more effective way of being. The phenomenon of wanting to remain well – in a culture that rarely permits enough time to recuperate from long working hours, commuting, and less-than-healthy living environments – is in itself deeply paradoxical. The concepts of "meaning and purpose" have been acknowledged as key factors in increasing psychological as well as physical resilience – something that is equally important whether it is related to work or to life in general.

MBCC can be used with individuals as well as with groups, and the client needs to be an active participant in his or her own coaching programme. The relevance and benefits of using a mindful approach to work and life are explored in relation to the client's presenting issue(s). The coach and client then decide on the best way of engaging in the

> **There is significant evidence that learning to experience life from moment to moment can create calm and well-being.**

MBCC process. Commitment is an essential requirement to ensure the best possible outcome, and the client is made aware of this right from the start. Some practices may only take a few minutes, but as James Walsh and I found during our study in 2008, clients can reap the benefits even from such short periods of practice. The learning of mindful awareness increases with each and every application: "A journey of a thousand miles starts with a single step!"

Acceptance and Commitment Therapy (ACT)

Stephen Hayes, the founder of ACT, believes that for psychological science to progress there needs to be a synergy between empiricism, theory, and observation.

How can someone commit to living an adventurous and purposeful life while suffering from emotional or physical pain? Acceptance and Commitment Therapy (ACT) is an active psycho-educational application of mindfulness, employing metaphors to communicate the multifaceted concept of mindfulness, as well as using cognitive behavioural exercises and homework to apply mindfulness to specific case-formulations. ACT is suited to one-on-one therapy, but can also be applied to groups. Research shows that it has better outcomes in decreasing depressive thoughts than CBT, and scores higher in pain management.

Acceptance and Commitment Therapy is an intellectually deep and complex therapy, focusing on "Six Core Processes":

- acceptance;

- cognitive diffusion;

- being in the present;

- looking at oneself as an observer;

- values and committed action to increase "psychological flexibility", which means being in touch with the present moment fully and on purpose;

- changing or persisting with behaviour in the service of the chosen principles.

Currently, traditional CBT has a much larger base of research than ACT, and this supports its validity. ACT focuses largely on addressing communication barriers, and thus can only be effective for clients who do not have language deficits, either in using or in understanding language.

According to Steven Hayes in *Get Out of Your Mind and Into Your Life*, "ACT

Below: *ACT is suited to one-on-one therapy, but it can also be applied in a group setting.*

is not about fighting your pain; it's about developing a willingness to embrace every experience life has to offer. It's not about resisting your emotions; it's about feeling them completely . . . (and choosing) . . . what matters to you most.

Above: *'Being mindful' is about embracing every experience life has to offer using all your senses: sound, touch, smell, taste, and vision.*

. . . The ultimate purpose of theory and philosophy is to guide the behaviour of the therapist through new territory."

Dialectical Behaviour Therapy (DBT)

DBT was originally developed by Marsha M Linehan, who worked as a researcher in the Department of Psychology at the University of Washington, where she looked after patients with borderline personality disorder (BPD).

Such patients tend to self-harm and suffer from intense mood-swings, and they also present a suicide risk. Linehan's treatment approach combined traditional cognitive interventions, in order to regulate emotion; it also aimed to help people cope with suffering and mental imbalance, and achieve acceptance and awareness, using methods largely derived from Buddhist meditative practices. It probably became the first therapy that demonstrated itself to be generally effective in treating BPD. It has also proved quite effective with sexual-abuse survivors and with clients who are dependent on drugs.

The main purpose of DBT is for the therapist to befriend the client. The psychotherapist aims to believe in and validate the client's feelings at any given time. Simultaneously the patient learns that some feelings and behaviours are maladaptive and destructive, and is shown various alternatives to them.

DBT consists of a variety of components and two specific parts of treatment. Part 1 looks at the one-to-one treatment aspect: the therapist and patient discuss the various problems that arise during the week, which are recorded on diary cards. The treatment follows a

hierarchy, with self-harm and suicidal behaviours taking priority. Next in terms of precedence are behaviours that are not self-harming, but that interfere with the treatment. The approach also investigates the client's quality of life. During the whole session the therapist and patient work towards improving life-skills. Part 2 is a group approach in which a number of clients in treatment meet once a week for two to three hours and practise how to use specific skills. These skills are broken down into four modules: core mindfulness skills; interpersonal effectiveness skills; emotion regulation skills; and distress tolerance skills. DBT also strongly recommends that all therapists attend weekly peer supervision and make themselves available to the client through telephone coaching between sessions. This is how the therapist becomes an intrinsic part of the client's world.

Both parts of the treatment are used together to avoid potential suicidal urges disrupting the group sessions. There is a general rule, when it comes to certain aspects of DBT, that applies to clients and therapists alike: "Any individual who misses four consecutive DBT meetings can no longer work with their pre-assigned DBT therapist, no matter how long they have been working together." This rule is used to encourage participation. It could, however, be interpreted as penalizing patients, since hospitalizations for medical purposes are not exempt. Anyone who wishes to use DBT needs to be really committed and willing to share what is happening in their lives. It has grown into a very popular treatment model since its early stages, although the training for therapists is extremely expensive.

Left: *Being still in this moment makes you more aware of the extraordinary experience of being alive.*

FINDING COMPASSION

One of the most important aspects of mindfulness-based therapies is the ability to perceive without judgement. Jon Kabat-Zinn names this as the first of his important attitudes towards mindfulness. As we all know, it is not easy to perceive without judging. We tend to name everything we perceive and, by giving a thing/experience a name, we often also give it a positive or negative meaning. This is not wrong or bad per se, for emotional labelling helps to orientate us in our environment, showing us where to place our attention, telling us what we like and dislike, and helping us to choose experiences in the future that are likely to give us a pleasant feeling. Unfortunately, we are so used to labelling and judging everything – and each experience that comes our way – that most of us have forgotten how to perceive without judging. Striving towards non-judgement leads towards compassion.

Left: *Years after her death, Mother Theresa continues to be a symbol for compassion. At the Home for the Dying that she founded in Calcutta, India, she and her sisters would care for the sick and the suffering, cleaning and feeding them until they passed on.*

Our daily routine without mindfulness

In our modern day-to-day-lives we tend to strive to achieve financial success and recognition, which often requires us to do more than one thing at a time – that is, multitask.

We plan our day while brushing our teeth in the morning. While having a hurried cup of coffee or tea for breakfast, we are mentally already in the car or on the train on the way to our job, preparing ourselves for the tasks the day will hold. Our mind also travels back to yesterday: what have we left unfinished?

Having arrived at work, we immediately switch to "job mode", dedicating our whole existence to solving whatever problem is put in front of us during the next eight to twelve hours. We may even like our job, like the way it challenges our intellect or how we feel when we achieve something. Perhaps we have a small break for lunch or coffee, a little chat with our colleagues, but then – sooner than anticipated – the working day is done and we switch back to "private mode" again.

On the way home we are either still thinking about what happened at work or we are planning the evening and weekend to come. So it sometimes happens that, when we are going through our daily chores on autopilot, we leave one of our bags on the train without realizing it, or find that another week has gone by without once calling our parents/children/friends. Furthermore, we are often oblivious to little signs within us that something is starting to go wrong.

Above: *The daily commute. Travelling to work can be very stressful. However, even in a crowded train you can focus on your breath mindfully.*

We are so occupied with things that *have been,* things that *will be*, and obstacles that *need to be moved out of the way* that we have forgotten to pay at least a little attention to the things that *are.* Many of us have never even really learned how to do that.

Being out of touch with the self

Everybody knows how a headache feels, or how painful a sore muscle can be (perhaps a muscle that we didn't even previously know existed).

But how many of us have ever given any attention to how our head feels when we do *not* suffer from a headache, when it is actually in a pleasant and well-functioning state?

Who gives a thought on a regular basis to their muscles while they are *not* in pain? It is hardly surprising that we tend

Below: *Mindfulness can assist you in reducing pain.*

FINDING COMPASSION

to become aware of problems only when they have already manifested, and long after the first signs of them have passed. We are not normally trained to listen to our bodies to familiarize ourselves with them, so that we know when they are in a balanced and wholesome state and when they are not. Learning how to respond to, and detect, changes early on and how to react wisely to avoid pain, danger, or long-term illness is another potential benefit of practising mindfulness.

It seems that, in this time of efficiency and success, we have forgotten to give ourselves the attention we need.

This is even truer when it comes to the mind and the soul – to one's psychological well-being. We expect everything to function well; we expect happiness in a relationship and satisfaction in a job. We notice extreme emotions such as anger, love, and hurt,

and very often we cannot cope with these feelings appropriately; cannot cope with them in a way that is true and supportive to us, as well as not offensive to others. It seems that, in this time of efficiency and success, we have forgotten to give ourselves the attention we need.

But why is this important? One of the keywords here is *value*. Giving a topic thought, attention, and time – something we seem to have so little of – means in the same moment giving this topic value. Things are considered important and worthy when we spend a lot of time doing/achieving them, and time is often considered to be the most precious commodity. So, as good parents, children, grandchildren, or friends, time is what we give to our loved ones. But we rarely present ourselves with this most valuable gift. We are on "autopilot" and more and more out of touch with ourselves.

How mindfulness can reconnect you to yourself

One thing that mindfulness aims to do is raise awareness to the actual moment – to thoughts, emotions, and body sensations that occur inside yourself at any given time.

Attention is paid to intentionally focusing on present-moment experiences, being in touch with the world through all your senses. The idea is to "give" yourself time, making yourself (and what you perceive at a given moment) important, without slipping into narcissism or egoism.

Below: *Peel your image from the mirror and meet the friend who has always been waiting for you.*

Giving time and thought to yourself for a change allows you to get to know yourself better. You can get into direct contact with emotions, body sensations, and thoughts that you are experiencing, because you can welcome all of it openly and without prejudice or superstition.

Giving time and thought to yourself for a change allows you to get to know yourself better.

In this way mindfulness encourages the connection that you have to yourself and the awareness that you have of yourself to grow stronger. On the other hand, mindfulness also provides you with just enough distance from your experiences, allowing you to respond wisely and in a way that is accepting and kind to yourself. Without experiencing distance from – for instance – physical or psychological pain, we tend to feel that we are nothing but pain. In such a case pain is everywhere, making it hard to see or perceive anything else.

It is easy to demonstrate this with a short experiment: take an A4 coloured folder and hold it as close to your face as possible. You will find it hard to see anything but the colour of the folder. It might not even be possible to recognize what it is that is taking over your visual field. But, as you move the folder away from your face, more and more details of your surroundings will become clear. All of a sudden it is obvious that this blue/red/yellow something that was blocking your way was in fact a folder, and that there is more than this folder. The folder has not changed; it is still the same folder, with the same size and colour. But, by giving it a little distance, it becomes recognizable, and something of a certain size that can be dealt with.

Finding compassion towards yourself and others

Mindfulness gives us exactly this distance. By giving ourselves time and thought – by allowing experiences of any kind to "simply be" – we can create this distance and thus form a real, close awareness of what is happening within ourselves, simply by valuing it as important.

Mindfulness enables us to better understand not only that we do/feel certain things at a given moment, but also *why* and *how* we experience it, without being overwhelmed, and without the danger of saying or doing things that we later regret.

Being aware of what is going on inside yourself naturally leads to more compassion towards yourself. If you are aware of how much you are upset or hurt in a given moment, without being overwhelmed by it and without judging or forbidding this experience,

Right: *Gently and kindly look after yourself as if you were your own best friend.*

you can learn to feel compassion towards yourself. You can decide which aspects of your experience you need to let be; you can let pass what needs to pass by, and you can change what perhaps needs to be

Above: *Give yourself a big hug, feel compassion for yourself, and enjoy the moment as best you can.*

changed. Mindfulness leads the way to self-compassion.

But mindfulness also leads to a better understanding of others.

Empathy towards yourself creates an improved ability to put yourself into the position of others – to accept and welcome with kindliness what they might be experiencing at a given moment. Having gone through a certain experience always makes it easier to understand others who might be in the same or a similar situation. So

---

Empathy towards yourself creates an improved ability to put yourself into the position of others.

---

mindfulness leads to an enhanced empathy towards others, which in turn leads to less conflict. Not only does mindfulness enable us to fine-tune empathy, but it also enables us to become aware of our strong feelings and have the freedom to respond to them, wisely and without hurting ourselves and others.

Last but not least, mindfulness and the acceptance that comes with it open the door to seeing aspects or moments of "failure" as part of life. Failure – like the folder in front of our face described on page 92 – is no longer overwhelming, no longer the essence of existence. It is like everything else: an experience that can be perceived, welcomed, and accepted, without having to give in to the perception of *being* a failure. It is put in the place where it can be dealt with like all other experiences. Parts of it may hurt and perhaps need changing. But, after all, failure is and remains part of the ever-changing flow of experience in our lives. The value of mindfulness giving us such insightful points of view in terms of our relationships – both towards ourselves and towards others – really cannot be overestimated.

FINDING COMPASSION

THE BLUE BALLOONS
A STORY ABOUT LETTING GO

This story shows how a lack of compassion for others can quench the joy of receiving gifts, and how clinging on to possessions and material things can eventually destroy the joy they might bring.

A little girl from a wealthy family is walking in the park with her parents when she sees a balloon seller.

"I want to have a blue balloon! A blue balloon is what I want!"

"Here you go, Rose!"

Now someone explains to her that the balloon contains certain gases that are lighter than air and, because of this, it floats.

"I want to let it go," she says impishly.

"Don't you want to give it to the poor little girl over there?"

"No, I want to let it go!" She lets it

go, watches it rise into the blue sky.

"Don't you regret not having given it to the poor little girl over there?"

"Yes, I would have rather given it to the poor little girl!"

"Here you are, give her this blue balloon!"

"No, I want to let this one go as well . . . see it fly up into the blue sky!" She simply lets it go. Then she is given a third blue balloon. She goes to the poor little girl of her own accord, gives her the balloon and says: "Now let it go!"

"No," says the poor little girl, looking excitedly at the balloon. In her room back at home the balloon flies up to the ceiling, where it remains for three days. Then it changes colour, gets darker, smaller, and finally drops to the floor like a little black bag. The poor little girl thinks: "I should have let it go outside in the garden, up into the blue sky. I could have watched

it fly away, watched it and watched it . . . "

In the meantime the rich little girl is given another 30 balloons in one go. She lets 20 of them fly up into the sky, and gives the remaining 10 to poor children. From this moment onwards she is never interested in balloons any more. "Those silly balloons . . . " she says.

The poor little girl, however, dreams: "I should have let it go, rise up into the blue sky. I would have watched it and watched it . . . "

ADAPTED FROM "IN THE PARK" BY PETER ALTENBERG

FINDING COMPASSION

Compassion for the difficult

There is a story told of a king who had three sons. Two of them were very good-looking and intelligent, and they were the stars of all the girls in the kingdom.

When they grew up, the king built them each a palace in the city and they soon found lovely princesses and lived happy lives.

The youngest son was neither very good-looking nor very clever. Everybody seemed to dislike him, and even the king himself found it difficult to see any good in him. When he turned 21, the king's advisers said, "Build him a little palace outside the city walls and send 50 soldiers with him to protect him." So this is what happened, and after a year the son sent a message to the king, which told him that the nomads outside the city wall had been difficult to hold at bay. So the advisers told the king to build him a palace 50 miles outside the city wall and give

him 100 soldiers to protect him. A year later the son sent another message: "We have been attacked many times and this is not a safe place to stay." The king once again consulted his advisers, who suggested building a castle on the other side of the river and sending 500 men to protect it.

Only when we turn towards our "self" with compassion and patience can we learn to respond wisely, rather than react with fear or in anger.

Of course this is what happened, and a year later the son wrote a letter to the king: "Father, we have lost over a hundred men by now, and I fear for the lives of the remaining soldiers and my own. Please help us." And the king said to his advisers, "Let him come home and live here in my palace with me. There is plenty of space for both of us. And let me learn how to love and protect my son, rather than waste lives and resources any longer."

Perhaps you could write down your own insights now, before you read the next paragraph.

The king could be seen as our "self", which shuts out the difficult, the ugly, the unlovable. And only when we turn towards our "self" with compassion and patience can we learn to respond wisely rather than react with fear or in anger.

Now read the poem on the right by the Sufi poet Rumi. After reading it, write down in your diary what emotions came up, which window you would rather open, and what kiss you are longing for with all your life?

There is some kiss we want with all our lives, the touch of

spirit on the body. Seawater begs the pearl to break its shell.

And the lily, how passionately it needs some wild darling! At

night, I open my window and ask the moon to come and press its

face against mine. Breathe into me. Close the language door and

open the love window. The moon won't use the door, only the window.

RUMI (TRANSLATED BY COLEMAN BARKS)

CASE STUDY
ANNA, 50

Looking back, there were signs of anxiety and depression when I was a child. At school I always felt different and was teased for my appearance and intellect – a common experience. There was little opportunity to talk about this at school or home, and I learned to accept bouts of intense crying and severe anxiety symptoms as normal. I became a shy and quiet adult with low self-esteem, although I was blessed with a sense of humour and intelligence.

These qualities took me to university to follow a career in medicine. This was a happy time, with many opportunities for hobbies, and friends who were also "different". Medicine was, however, an extremely stressful course in later years, and at the start of my fourth year I suffered my first episode of depression. I recognized the symptoms that I had been studying and went to see my doctor, who prescribed antidepressants. Within a few weeks I was feeling better and was able to complete my course. My doctor advised me to take the medication for longer, but, aware of the stigma of mental illness, I stopped taking the antidepressants after the minimum recommended six months.

I continued with my medical career and went into research. Away from university life there were fewer opportunities for hobbies, and I continued to push myself to work hard and became a workaholic. I didn't know how to unwind, and subsequently suffered my second episode of depression following a period of intense stress at work. I was prescribed a different antidepressant this time, by a new doctor, and I was left with mild symptoms, though I didn't realize it at the time, and gained weight. I had very low self-esteem, but was able to function. Eventually I requested a referral for Cognitive Behavioural Therapy, which helped, but it wasn't enough. I then began to research alternative options for myself.

To a large extent I withdrew from the world over the years that followed, lost in a world of books and medical writing. I felt safe here, unlikely to be hurt, and I spent a lot of time alone. In many ways this time was like a long retreat. I emerged with immense knowledge and understanding of the brain, Buddhist philosophy, meditation, and some tools to manage my challenging emotions. It was during this time that I became pregnant with my first child. I was referred to a specialist mental-health team, due to my history of depression, and this caused me significant anxiety. My doctor was not surprised that I suffered my third episode of depression after

the birth of my first child, though fortunately without any psychosis. I was again prescribed antidepressants and this time I stayed on the treatment for a significant period of time.

After I discovered Jon Kabat-Zinn's book, *Full Catastrophe Living*, I became determined to train as a mindfulness teacher. I participated in an eight-week mindfulness course, followed by a week-long retreat –

a challenging requirement that would take me away from my young family. However, it was an amazing experience and I remember not wanting it to end. I felt so much peace and compassion there, and I was in tears on the final day. Thich Nhat Hanh noticed and asked his monastics to sing their farewell song, "No Coming, No Going", which was extremely comforting. There followed more

reading of books by this inspiring human being, and further retreats, deepening my understanding and practice of mindfulness. Eventually I was ready to attend mindfulness teacher-development training.

Over the past ten years any residual symptoms of anxiety and depression have reduced, little by little, with regular mindfulness practice. I feel privileged to be able to pass on to others what I have learned, and to share the journeys of many special people. I organized a party for my fiftieth birthday recently and felt so happy – dancing, carefree, and surrounded by close friends and family. With mindfulness, I noticed these feelings, and my thoughts turned to: "Thank you mindfulness, for giving me my life back."

PART 2

Mindfulness in practice

THE ESSENTIAL MEDITATIONS

I n Part 1 of this book you were introduced to the history, research, application, and use of mindfulness and mindfulness practices. Part 2 will help you find and experiment with a variety of meditation exercises that may appeal to you. They follow the order that would be taught on a course such as the eight-session MBCT course (see pages 220–303). However, it is up to you whether you wish to follow this order (one meditation for six days a week) or create your own programme. "There is no right or wrong way of doing this, there is only *your way* of doing this" as Jon Kabat-Zinn has said.

Below: *Take time to experiment with a variety of meditation exercises to find out what suits you.*

Making yourself comfortable

You should start by selecting a special space at home to which you will return regularly to practise mindfulness. Your subconscious will remember that this is the place for peace and stillness.

If you have a spare room to do this in, that is wonderful. However, any quiet corner – for example, in your bedroom or kitchen – can be just as useful. The space you select needs to help you feel undisturbed and calm.

I would avoid rooms where you work on a computer or watch TV, as they tend to be unconsciously connected to "active" thinking and doing. However, if your living space is limited, one idea is to cover any technical equipment with a pretty cloth, to create the quiet space that your mind needs for entering inner stillness. It can also be helpful to dim the lights.

The invitation is to use your imagination and your personal preferences to design a peaceful area. You may want to include the following items:

Above: *Create a space for mindfulness at home.*

- A little table with a candle

- A photo of a calm and serene place

- Fresh flowers and/or shells, stones, dried flowers, and so on, that you have collected yourself.

Choose whatever gives you a sense of gladness and serenity.

You will also require:

- A supportive chair, a stool or a cushion to sit on (a *zafu* is a meditation cushion used in the Japanese Zen tradition); or a yoga mat, blanket, or rug, if you want to lie on the floor.

- A shawl or a blanket to keep yourself snug.

I will offer you a variety of theories and ideas throughout this book, but a large part of your learning will come from practising meditation yourself. Certain instructions are constant in most meditations. They are to:

- Sit with dignity (upright, but not stiffly)

- Focus on your feet being connected with the ground

- Breathe naturally

- Observe the natural in- and out-breath, allowing your breath to just happen

- Bring your mind back from wandering off, and reconnect it to your breath or any other focus of your choice.

To practise meditation effectively it really helps to feel at ease, so choose postures that are conducive to feeling calm and aware: only sit cross-legged on the floor if that feels comfortable

Above: *A selection of the different postures you can choose from for practising meditation.*

to you. Alternatively you can sit on a chair, against the wall, kneel, or stand – whatever works for you.

Having the right posture is really important to enable you to focus on the mindful exercise, and for your well-being. If you are sitting on a chair, make sure that your feet are firmly on the floor; do not cross your legs, to avoid getting pins and needles. If the chair feels a little high, a cushion underneath your feet will help you feel more grounded and solid. Sit upright and with deliberate awareness. Your lower

Below: *As you relax during meditation, your body temperature will drop. Because of this, using a blanket or a shawl is highly recommended.*

back can be aligned with the back of the chair; from the waist upwards, however, straighten your back so that it supports itself (if you learn to strengthen your pelvic muscles, you will be able to support yourself better). Keep your neck loose and relaxed and your chin slightly tucked under. Rest your hands in your lap, with the palms pointing either down or up. A shawl or a blanket around your shoulders will keep you snug and warm.

If you have chosen to rest on the floor, lie down on a yoga mat, thick blanket, or rug, and try a thin cushion under your head. Let your legs fall apart (alternatively, you can make a

triangle with them, by placing the feet on the floor, with your knees pointing towards the ceiling). Your arms should lie gently on the floor, with the palms of your hands pointing towards the ceiling. Again use a blanket or shawl to cover yourself and keep you warm.

Feeling peaceful and calm is an important part of making yourself comfortable before starting. In reality, however, it is not always possible to find total silence. So whatever sounds occur in the background, try to let them pass by without focusing on them.

It can be very helpful to "make a date with yourself" for your meditation practice. Note it down in your diary. I recommend times when you're neither too hungry nor too full, or too tired. Ideally, wear comfortable clothes such as leggings or loose trousers and a T-shirt and warm socks. If you feel mentally restless, or have "to-do lists" running through your mind, start with some mindful movements (see pages 150–84) before settling down to meditate.

CASE STUDY
ELSA, 76, FELLOW MEDITATOR

As I am a diabetic, excess adrenalin can have adverse effects on my blood sugar levels. I found the information on how our minds control the chemicals that our bodies produce fascinating and life changing. Since I attended mindfulness training I have become much more aware of my body's signals. This has enabled me to avoid sugar highs and lows and has resulted in my blood pressure being more balanced. I have reconnected to my love of music and photography and have started to sort out my slides and recordings from 30 years of collecting. I am spending more time in the garden and have created a little "paradise" to which I can retreat when I need to. There are many moments of joy and I have become much more alert to when I am experiencing them.

What can get in the way of mindfulness practice

The following is only a selection of "hindrances" that can get in the way of your mindfulness practice. You may find your own, and could note them down in your diary. Awareness is the first step towards freedom and change.

Mindfulness requires ongoing endeavour

Mindfulness takes determination, but the good news is that the longer you practise, the easier it gets and the more joyful your life may become.

Initially your thoughts will be scattered all over the place. You

might feel helpless, but the more you focus on being fully connected to where you find yourself right now, the easier it will be to find peace of mind in the moment – even in a challenging moment, for we know "this too will pass" and "everything passes at last".

Mindfulness is best practised throughout your day. It is not just for when you sit down and meditate. Focus on being mindful of your thoughts when you are doing everyday tasks, and you may find that it will become

Above: *Practising mindfulness requires ongoing endeavour, even when the going gets tough.*

easier to remain aware, even when things get tough and demanding.

There may be distractions

When you're on your journey to becoming more mindful it seems as if the universe starts throwing things at you, just to give you challenges. These distractions might be problems in your life, challenging relationships, or old negative beliefs from your past.

These are great opportunities to practise present-moment awareness. All the "battles" will help you become stronger and more in tune with yourself. The problems that we face are teachers in disguise, and they may be there to help you grow and realize who you truly are. (Try reading "The Guest House" by Rumi, see page 273.)

Progress doesn't always come quickly (and what is progress anyway?)

Progress may seem agonizingly slow at times. There will be moments when you find yourself attached to things and situations that you desire, which can make it near-impossible to be fully in the present. We all experience this sometimes. The more we want something, the more we tend to fixate on not having it and wanting to get it.

Try saying the following aphorism to yourself, to remind yourself to be grateful for what you have right now: "If I manage to release the attachment,

Above: *The journey to mindfulness will present many opportunities to practise present-moment awareness.*

and focus on being grateful for what I have in the moment, my life seems to shift to a more peaceful space."

You may want to throw in the towel

As on any worthwhile journey, you may be tempted to give up on many occasions. But it is at the times when

you feel most frustrated that you are often on the verge of a breakthrough.

Our lives are very similar to the seasons. We go through cold, dark winters and joyful, expanding summers. It all comes and goes. It's part of the ebb and flow of life. When you realize that the challenging times are there to help you grow, you will automatically feel more peaceful and relaxed.

Too many fixed goals may challenge your mindfulness practice

Having goals is a fantastic thing – essential, even – but when you become overly attached to them, you may find they distract you from your mindfulness practice. You will know that you are too attached to something when you start feeling frustrated, angry, and negative.

Attachment muddles our clarity. You are probably pursuing your goals because you believe they will make you happy – remember that, when you start letting your goals pull you into a stressful state of mind. All you

---

When you are practising mindfulness, remember that there is nowhere to arrive at. If you focus on what is going on right now, the rest will take care of itself.

---

need to do is focus on the good things around you, and you may indeed start feeling the happiness that you think you need to chase. This will make you much happier in the long term and, of course, right now too.

You might forget that the journey is the destination

Most people miss the fact that the reward lies in the journey. Have you ever noticed that when you reach a

goal, it is not as exciting as you thought it would be? Sure, it feels great to hit a milestone, but if you do not replace that goal with another one, you will soon find yourself feeling unfulfilled. That's because we are goal-seeking beings. Humans need goals so that they can feel a sense of purpose.

It is on the journey that we learn, grow, and become better. When you are practising mindfulness, remember that there is nowhere to arrive at. If you focus on what is going on right now, the rest will take care of itself.

Now and then you'll want to be anywhere but in the "now"

Even the most enlightened masters on Earth have to deal with difficult situations and chaotic thoughts. The difference is that they have learned to accept the moment for what it is. When you do this, you become the guardian of your inner space, which is the only way to feel good inside and to find peace of mind right now.

THE BODY SCAN

FOR INNER STILLNESS,
SELF-AWARENESS, A CALM
MIND, GROUNDING
YOURSELF WHEN ANXIOUS,
AND BETTER SLEEP

1 Go to your special meditation place, switch off any phones, and sit or lie down comfortably. Perhaps initially set an alarm clock or timer to 30 minutes. Whether you are lying or sitting down, gently cover yourself with a light blanket or shawl to avoid feeling cold. If you choose, you may close your eyes or keep them in soft-focus (half-open and unfocused). Should you experience any discomfort while lying down, try placing your feet flat on the floor with your knees pointing upwards, and a rolled-up towel or cushion under your lower back for support.

2 There is no need to move at all throughout the whole Body Scan practice. As best you can, just "switch on a torchlight" from within, shining it onto the particular body part you are focusing on at each moment. If necessary, notice your wandering mind, acknowledge where it has gone, and then patiently escort it back to the journey through your body. If your mind wanders off again, accept the situation and continue wherever your awareness picks up.

3 Bring your attentiveness slowly to your body, feeling the points of contact that it makes with the floor, rug, mat, or chair. Start with the intention of "falling awake", in order to sense your body in a new way. Perhaps you notice the pressure between your feet and legs on the rug or floor, and your back touching the surface of the chair. Now bring your awareness to your shoulders, checking mindfully whether they feel tense or loose. And notice the feeling of your hands resting in your lap or on the floor.

4 Place one of your hands on your chest or stomach and notice how it rises on the in-breath and falls on the out-breath. Don't feel as if you need to change your breathing deliberately, by deepening or lengthening it in any way. Just allow your body to breathe of its own accord – it knows exactly how to do this! – and accept the invitation to experience the texture of each breath fully as it comes and goes.

5 Observe whether each breath is different – longer or shorter, deeper or shallower – and after a while perhaps also the pauses between each in- and out-breath. See each breath as a new beginning. If your mind wanders off into planning, analyzing, or other forms of thought, gently become aware of this wandering and then patiently guide your focus back to your breathing. Even if you have to go through this process every few

seconds, there is no need to get impatient or frustrated, although if you do feel these emotions, that's okay too. The nature of the mind is such that it tends to jump about like a monkey from branch to branch, and everyone has plenty of automatic (jumpy) thoughts throughout every day. They are present most of the time, lurking just beneath the surface of awareness, although before you actually start practising mindfulness you are probably not even aware of their existence. So for now just accept this fact, and feel content when you notice the wandering mind, for only a mindful observer can do that. Then bring your attention back to the anchor of breathing in and out, again and again.

6 Put your hand gently back into its original position after a while, and change your focus to your body as a whole. In a moment you are going to take a journey in which truly inhabiting your body – not just your brain – may help you get clues about your well-being, state of mood, and health, in a fresh and immediate way.

7 Guide your awareness to your left foot when you feel ready to continue. Start with the left big toe, then the left little toe, the toes in between, and even the spaces between the toes. Feel them, sense them, or simply know that they are there.

8 Choose now to switch your focus to the rest of your left foot: the sole, the instep, the heel, the upper part, all the little bones, blood vessels, and tendons, and then the left ankle. Feel these parts in their entirety and just know that they are present.

9 Gently move your focus of attention upwards to your calf and shin, knee and kneecap, then focus on your outer and inner thigh. Thus, having scanned your whole left leg, I invite you to breathe in mindfully, and mentally send the breath all the way down in your left leg to your toes. On the out-breath you may choose to release any tightness or discomfort from this area. Repeat this breathing in and out a few more times. If you consider the idea of "breathing into your leg" a little unusual, try picturing your blood carrying fresh oxygen to your leg on the in-breath.

10 Consider how your left leg (through which you have journeyed) is feeling now, versus the right one. Are you aware of any differences in sensation, such as a tingling in one and not in the other; or heaviness

versus lightness, coolness versus heat, and so on? Remember that no right or wrong answer applies, so whether a difference is or is not apparent doesn't matter. Just gently bring your awareness to your experience and observe with interest whatever you find. Now let go mentally of your left leg.

11 When you feel ready to continue, guide your awareness to your right foot. Start with the right big toe, then the right little toe, the toes in between, and even the spaces between the toes. Feel them, sense them, or simply know that they are there.

12 Choose now to switch your focus to the rest of your right foot, the sole, the instep, the heel, the upper part, all the little bones, blood vessels and tendons, and then the right ankle, feeling these parts or just knowing that they are present. Gently move your focus of attention upwards to your calf and shin, knee and kneecap, now focusing on your outer and inner thigh. Thus, having scanned your whole right leg, I invite you once again to breathe in mindfully, and mentally send the breath all the way down your right leg to your toes. On the out-breath you may choose to release any tightness or discomfort from this area. Repeat this breathing in and out a few more times.

13 Consider how your right leg (through which you have just journeyed) is feeling now, versus the left one. Are you aware of any differences in sensation, such as a tingling in one and not in the other; or heaviness versus lightness, and so on? Remember once again that no right or wrong answer applies, so whether a difference is or is not apparent doesn't matter. Just gently bring your awareness to your experience and observe with interest whatever you find.

14 Pause for a moment and allow your legs to recede into the background of your awareness after completing the passage, bringing your torso to centre-stage.

15 Focus in turn on your sitting bones and buttocks, hips and reproductive areas, stomach and navel, chest and ribcage, collar bones and shoulders, upper, middle, and lower back, and your spine – vertebra by vertebra – being present in every moment.

16 Now start concentrating on some of your vital organs, starting with the heart and then the lungs, liver, stomach and digestive tract, kidneys, adrenal glands, and urinary tract. Of course you can add any other body part that seems relevant to you. Notice that you have now scanned your whole torso, gently breathing into it and allowing any tension or discomfort to be released on the out-breath. Continue repeating this process a few more times.

17 Now turn your awareness to your left arm and hand, starting with the fingertips and then the thumb, pointer finger, middle finger, ring finger, and little finger. Then shift your focus to the palm of your left hand, the back of the hand and the knuckles, moving up to the left wrist, forearm, and upper arm. Breathe into your left arm and hand on the next in-breath, releasing any tension or discomfort in your arm on the out-breath. After repeating this action, breathing in and out a couple more times, move your attention to the right arm and hand.

18 Start again with the fingertips and then the thumb, pointer finger, middle finger, ring finger, and little finger. Then shift your focus to the palm of your right hand, and the back and knuckles, moving up to the right wrist, forearm, and upper arm. Breathe into your right arm and hand on the next in-breath, releasing any tension or discomfort on the out-breath.

19 Next shift your awareness to the neck and head area, starting with your neck and throat, cheeks and chin, mouth, lips, teeth, tongue, and gums. Continue with your ears and earlobes, nose and nostrils, and eyes: sockets, eyeballs, lashes, lids, and brows. Then move your awareness to your forehead, temples, and the back and crown of your head. Imagine now a blowhole in the crown of your head. Breathe in deeply through this opening, sending clear and refreshing energy to each cell of your body, releasing tension or discomfort on the out-breath. Repeat a few more times and then return to observing your breathing. You could use the recorded sound of a singing bowl or *tingsha* to finish the practice.

20 Start stretching, wriggling your toes and fingers, then opening your. After a couple of minutes, if you're lying on the floor, turn to your left side and then, very slowly, come to a sitting and then a standing position.

THE ESSENTIAL MEDITATIONS

THE BODY SWEEP

A SHORTER PRACTICE FOR WHEN YOU HAVE JUST A FEW MINUTES

1 Standing or sitting, feel your feet firmly on the ground and, from head to toe, mentally sweep through your entire body. Should you become aware of areas that feel tense and tight, breathe into them and release any discomfort on the out-breath.

GRATITUDE BODY SCAN

A TOOL TO HELP YOU FEEL GOOD, BEAUTIFUL AND HAPPY WITH YOURSELF

1 First of all, write down a list of all the parts of your body and the aspects of your behaviour that you are not happy with. Then make another list of all the parts of your body and the behaviours that you think are good enough and that make you feel satisfied. Make this an ongoing exercise – keep adding to it.

2 Now lie down on your bed or on a rug on the floor and cover yourself with a blanket. Perhaps light a candle or an incense stick. Allow yourself a good 20–30 minutes, choosing a place and a time when you will not be disturbed.

3 Start with your feet and then, slowly and mindfully, work all the way up your body. Focus on sensing the body part in question, and give thanks for how well it has served you. Do not differentiate between the so-called "pretty" parts and those you would rather change. Thank each body part for what it has enabled you to do. For example, thank your feet for making it possible to walk.

4 Add to your Gratitude Body Scan (GBS) the beneficial actions that you can perform because of the functionality of the different parts of your body. So, when feeling your hands, for example, stay a little while just sensing them and then say, "Thank you, hands, for helping me to bake cookies, which give joy to my friends and neighbours."

5 Every GBS will be a little different. As best you can, let each one unfold moment by moment; and the more you notice how well parts of your body have assisted you, the less you are likely to focus purely on their look.

MUSICAL BODY PRACTICE

FOR THOSE WHO LIKE MUSIC AND LIFE, OR WANT TO RECONNECT WITH THEM

We have forgotten that within us is the bubbling presence of life – or God, if you prefer. We can learn to feel this vibrant and joyful energy, and this will help us to remember that we are loved. In fact, this simple exercise will help us to be present within ourselves; our bodies like to feel the presence of our mind, just as a child can relax when it feels the loving presence of its mother/father/care-giver. Performing the Musical Body Practice can help you to relax and represents the first step towards loving yourself. It takes approximately 20–30 minutes.

Do this practice first thing in the morning, or in the evening before you go to bed. Perform it to the sound of gentle, flowing instrumental music. Choose a piece that you really feel connected to; or maybe try different pieces. You are invited to sense the music that you are listening to in each part of your body, and then in your entire body. Stay with each body part that is mentioned for about one minute (or six to eight breaths). Remember: keep to intervals of one minute; and do both sides of the legs/arms together.

1 Start listening to your chosen music and sensing it in:

- Both feet
- Both ankles
- Both calves
- Both knees
- Both thighs
- The reproductive organs and sitting bones
- Hips
- Abdomen
- Chest
- Both shoulders
- Both upper arms
- Both elbows

- Both forearms
- Both wrists
- Both hands
- Shoulder girdle/both shoulders
- Neck
- Face
- Head
- And the entire body.

2 When you have completed this practice and have felt the music on a cellular level, stay with the sensations a little longer. If at all possible, just breathe and be. Only when you feel ready, write down mindfully in your journal what you experienced (it's for your eyes only).

TEN-MINUTE SOUND MEDITATION

FOR COMING INTO STILLNESS AND AWARENESS, AND LETTING GO OF RUMINATIVE THINKING

1 When you feel ready, go to your special meditation place, switch off any phones, and sit down comfortably. Perhaps initially set an alarm clock or timer to ten minutes. Bear in mind that the anchor of attention for this practice is the *awareness of sound*.

2 Bring your awareness to the surface that your feet are resting on and what it feels like. Perhaps observe the temperature of your feet and the surrounding air, the roughness or smoothness of the floor, cushion, or carpet that you've placed your feet on; even bring your awareness to the sensation of the socks or slippers you may be wearing. In the same way, scan your whole body, noticing the areas that are in contact with the floor or the chair, or your hands resting in your lap or on your legs.

3 Close your eyes, if this feels comfortable, or keep them in soft-focus, gradually bringing your awareness to any sounds that you can hear. These sounds may be inside you, inside the room, or coming from outside. Here are a few examples to get you started:

- Your stomach rumbling
- The floor creaking
- Footsteps outside
- Cars, planes and motorbikes
- Voices
- Animals moving or communicating
- The wind and the rain.

Don't worry about labelling or naming these sounds consciously; instead, just allow them to arise in your awareness and pass through it. Don't cling onto pleasant sounds, judge unpleasant ones, or try to interpret unfamiliar sounds; just accept any sound for what it is, receiving it with interest and curiosity.

4 Imagine that you are a child hearing all of these patterns of sound for the very first time. Simply listen to them with inquisitiveness but without judgement, so that you feel the vibration of the sounds and respond to them emotionally, rather than evaluating or intellectually understanding them.

5 As in all mindfulness meditations, every so often you are going to find yourself back in "thinking mode": planning, wondering, daydreaming, or just thinking that you really liked one sound and disliked another. As soon as you become aware of having involuntarily switched focus, observe where your mind has wandered off to and, without judgement, begin to escort it back to listening to sound.

Don't worry about how often you need to return it; just gently remind yourself that the nature of the mind is to jump from tree to tree, rather like a squirrel.

6 Try to focus on the distance or closeness of a sound, its pitch, strength, length, its coming and going, and whether or not it repeats itself. Sooner or later you may become aware of the spaces between the sounds – in other words, "the sound of silence" – and you may even notice that your hearing appears more acute, more focused. Enjoy this feeling, and remember it for future meditative exercises; the ability to "discover" silence is a useful one indeed.

7 Notice the sound of the timer or alarm after ten minutes, returning your focus gently to the sensations in your body and to the points of contact with the surface that you are sitting or lying on. Connecting to the floor, with your feet firmly planted and your body feeling grounded, slowly open your eyes.

TEN-MINUTE SIGHT MEDITATION
FOR CALM, FOCUS, AND EXPERIENCING LIFE AS A MIRACLE

1 Go to your special meditation place, switch off any phones, and sit down comfortably. Perhaps initially set an alarm clock or timer to ten minutes. Bear in mind throughout that the anchor of attention for this practice is the *awareness of sight*.

2 Bring your awareness to the surface that your feet are resting on and what it feels like. Perhaps observe the temperature of your feet and the surrounding air, the roughness or smoothness of the floor, cushion, or carpet you have placed your feet on; even bring awareness to the sensation of the socks or slippers you may be wearing. In the same way, scan your whole body and notice the areas that are in contact with the floor or the chair, or your hands resting in your lap or on your legs. This practice can be done standing, if you wish.

3 Find one object of attention that you will be viewing for the next ten minutes. It could be something you can place in your hand, like an ornament, a rock, a semi-precious stone, or some fruit; alternatively you can choose to view the single leaf of a plant, a picture on the wall, or even a window and whatever things you can see through it. If you choose the last example, make sure that you do not let your vision move about, but stay with the first image you picked up by looking though your chosen window. This practice will help you see the minutiae of life. Even a white wall will become interesting and transparent, when you give your eyes time to settle – you may see the different brushstrokes, thickness of paint, or a little unevenness here and there.

4 Imagine being a child and seeing this object for the first time ever. You need only respond to the "picture" emotionally, rather than evaluating or intellectually understanding it.

5 As in all mindfulness meditations, every so often you are going to find yourself back in "thinking mode": planning, wondering, daydreaming. As soon as you become aware of having involuntarily switched focus, observe where your mind has wandered off to and, without judgement, begin to escort it back to just seeing and viewing. Don't worry about how often you need to return the mind to your chosen object; just gently remind yourself that the nature of the mind is to be unsteady and overactive at times.

6 Sometimes you may notice that your sense of seeing appears more acute, more focused. Enjoy this feeling, and remember it for future meditative exercises; the ability to "discover" a single dot or brushstroke, for example, may be a useful skill to hone in on.

7 Notice the sound of the timer or alarm after ten minutes, returning your focus gently to the sensations in your body and the points of contact with the surface that you are sitting or lying on. As you connect to the floor, with your feet firmly planted and your body feeling grounded, slowly open your eyes and reorientate yourself.

MINDFUL BREATHING EXERCISE

FOR MOVING INTO CALM
AND LETTING GO OF
ANGER OR ANXIETY

1 Go to your special meditation place, switch off any phones, and sit down comfortably. You may choose to experiment with sitting on a chair or on a rug or cushion on the floor, either kneeling on the cushion or sitting with crossed legs. If you are kneeling, make sure that you put a soft towel underneath each shin; if you cross your legs, support your knees with small rolled-up towels or cushions, so that you sit on a "tripod", so to speak. Perhaps initially set an alarm clock or timer to 15 minutes.

2 When you feel ready, place yourself in a comfortable yet dignified posture, with your spine erect and self-supporting and your chin angled slightly down. Allow your shoulders to rest in a comfortable, neutral position (neither falling forward, nor thrust backwards), so as not to inhibit your breathing in any way. Close your eyes gently; or by all means keep them in soft-focus (half-closed), if you prefer, resting on a point on the floor about a metre in front of you.

3 Bring your awareness to certain body sensations, by focusing your attention on the touch or contact that your body makes with the floor and whatever you are sitting on. Spend a few minutes exploring these sensations.

4 Now turn your attention to your abdomen. Feel it rising/expanding gently on the in-breath and falling/deflating on the out-breath. Focus on your breathing, "being with" each in-breath for its duration and with each out-breath for its duration, as if riding on the waves of your own breathing.

5 Sooner or later you may notice a little pause after each in-breath and after each out-breath. You may also become aware of the unique nature of each breath. Sometimes you may breathe longer and deeper, which may signify a state of calmness, and at other times you may breathe shorter and shallower. There is no need to ponder on these differences; simply accept

that each breath is a unique moment and just allow your body to breathe.

6 If your mind wanders off, as it probably will, gently and without judgement notice where it has wandered to, and then bring your attention back to your abdomen and the feeling of the breath coming in and out. Even if this wandering happens a thousand times, gently and without criticism bring your mind back to the breath every time, no matter what it becomes preoccupied with. Becoming aware that your mind has wandered, and bringing it back to the breath, is just as important as remaining aware of the breath.

7 Let go of the anchor of awareness – your breath – after about 15 minutes or so, and slowly focus on those parts of the body that are in touch with the surface you are sitting on. Deeply ground yourself and feel rooted in your seat, before gently opening your eyes.

AWARENESS OF SOUND, BODY SENSATION, AND BREATH MEDITATION

FOR DEEPENING AWARENESS AND CALM SETTLING

1 Go to your special meditation place, switch off any phones, and sit down comfortably. Perhaps initially set an alarm clock or timer to 15 minutes. This exercise is an invitation for you to explore the sensations in your body and the awareness of your breathing. Slowly but surely you learn to become your own guide and to follow whatever intuitively helps your mind and body to settle.

2 When you feel ready, sit with your spine erect and let your shoulders drop. As with all the sitting exercises, your aim is to adopt a dignified posture, with your head, neck, and back vertically aligned. This position manifests the inner attitudes of self-reliance, self-acceptance, patience, and alertness that you are trying to cultivate. Close your eyes, if doing so feels comfortable.

3 Bring your awareness to any sound that you notice in your environment. There is no need to judge sound as pleasant or unpleasant – it simply comes and goes.

4 Now bring your awareness to the sensations in your body. Focus your attention on the sensations of touch and contact that your body makes with the floor and whatever you are sitting on, and spend a little while exploring these feelings.

5 Then focus your attention on your stomach, feeling it rise gently on the in-breath and fall on the out-breath. Keep the focus on your breathing, "being with" each in-breath for its full duration and with each out-breath for its full duration. As you are sitting,

it will feel as if your stomach is moving away from the spine on the in-breath and towards the spine on the out-breath. You may become aware of some discomfort – explore it with curiosity rather than fear. You may want to breathe into it and see what happens.

6 Notice when your mind wanders off into thinking, pondering, and worrying. Softly note what took your attention away, and then gently escort your focus back to your stomach and the feeling of the breath coming in and out. Repeat this process however

many times it happens, no matter what the mind becomes preoccupied with. Congratulate yourself on noticing these wanderings, because that means you are being mindful.

7 Focus on your breath and the sensation of your body touching the surface you are sitting on. Expand your body awareness even further, noticing all the areas that are involved when breathing, and even picturing all the cells of your body breathing in and out. Deeply ground yourself and feel rooted in your seat, before gently opening your eyes.

THE ESSENTIAL MEDITATIONS

SITTING WITH DIFFICULT THOUGHTS MEDITATION

FOR LETTING GO OF FEAR, SELF-DISLIKE, NEGATIVE THOUGHTS, AND ANGER

This meditation is one in which you invite thoughts to arise. The approach here is decidedly different from allowing thoughts to rumble on or draw you into some kind of story. All the while you remain in control. Here you look at your thoughts as if you are an external observer, seeing them for what they are: events of the mind, and not necessarily true, false, or important in any way.

In order to achieve such a detached position, I will make a few suggestions below that will enable you to observe your thoughts without needing to act or react:

- **You're watching your thoughts as clouds in the sky.** Your thoughts are there one moment and then slowly passing through your awareness.

- **You're standing on a bridge across a river.** You watch leaves, which represent your thoughts, floating beneath you and away.

- **You're looking at your thoughts written on individual balloons that you are holding.** You read each one and then let it go and float away. Repeat this with the next balloon, and so on.

- **You're watching a presentation of slides, in which each slide represents a thought.** When you've seen each slide, swiftly click on to the next one.

- **You're in a theatre.** Actors representing your thoughts come for an audition; listen to each actor briefly, then thank him or her and move on to the next.

- **You're in a sushi bar.** On the conveyor belt you observe the little plates passing. Each plate has a thought written on it; let it pass by, even if it returns after a while.

- **You're standing at a train station, watching a long train go by.** Each carriage has one of your thoughts written on it.

- **You pick up a fluffy dandelion and blow hard at the clock.** Let your thoughts be blown away by each seed.

- **You hold a bottle of soap bubbles.** When you blow, each bubble is a thought you are letting go of.

If you prefer, you can create your own metaphor for acknowledging your thoughts, but not getting involved with them. When you have a framework in mind, proceed as described here.

1 To begin your meditation, sit in your meditation space, having decided how long you will spend meditating and having set an alarm clock to help

you finish on time. Gently close your eyes, if this feels okay for you. Now start focusing on the sense of your body as a whole. Bring awareness to the space you are taking up, and the connection points that you can feel between your body and the ground or chair that you are sitting on. With time you may notice your mind settling and focusing more and more on your chosen anchor of attention, such as sound or body awareness. You may even focus on the skin – the largest organ of your body – and how it feels: whether it is cool or warm and whether the differences in temperature are the same on both sides of your body.

2 Allow thoughts to arise in your awareness. They may do so or they may not; just let yourself just be, with or without thoughts, moment by moment. Whenever a thought appears, use your pre-selected metaphor from the list given above. Give the thought space, look at it, and then let it go without needing to understand it fully or change anything. For now you're simply bringing awareness to the patterns of thoughts that may appear in this particular practice.

3 Invite difficult or stressful thoughts to arise in the safety and security of this meditation. I am not suggesting that you deal here with thoughts of a traumatic nature. But perhaps you could look at an argument with a friend that needs resolving: just observe how both of you acted.

4 End the meditation at the sound of your alarm bell. Before you stop, ground yourself properly once more, and let go of any content of the meditation before you open your eyes. Have the intention not to continue ruminating on a thought any longer, but to let it be for now. You can always decide to return to "the problem" in your next meditation.

SITTING WITH "SPACIOUS AWARENESS" EXERCISE
FOR MORE ADVANCED MEDITATORS

This exercise is also called "Choiceless Awareness". In this practice you don't anchor your awareness in one particular way. It's a free-flowing meditation, which has its own beauty and is different every time you practise it. You can see it as allowing the mind to observe whatever arises during the meditation. Issues that have been deeply repressed may begin to rise to the surface, providing you with the opportunity to address them consciously.

Choiceless Awareness may create a quality of mind that is free from making judgements, decisions, or generating observations as it meets "sense experiences". It assists the mind to respond to each new moment without the burden of its past history or of making future projections. When the mind no longer clings to anything – not even the idea of "not clinging" – you may realize, suddenly or gradually, that you already are what you have been searching for.

This means that all that you are – even the imperfect, stumbling actions you engage in – already holds the key to beauty and kindness. This concept may be an odd one to grasp, but think of it as having the intention to achieve a greater sense of spaciousness and as sitting with determination, while also being open to different "anchors of attention" and awareness.

1 Sit with open awareness. You can focus on your breath for a while.

2 When a sound becomes inviting, sit with sounds for a while. Move (don't rush) from one anchor to the next, whenever your awareness pulls you towards it. In the end you will probably embrace several – or all – of the senses.

BREATHING SPACE – EMERGENCY MEDITATION
FOR EVERYONE IN NEED

When life is challenging, the brain tends to forget the useful lessons it learned previously. Basically, adrenaline and cortisol affect areas of our memory so that we cannot access the necessary interventions. This is why it is most helpful to do the Breathing Space practice three times a day, so that you know it by heart, however taxing life may be. It can be a useful way to break away from a rotten mood or anxious emotions, and can help calm you before a presentation or an interview, for example. In summary, the Breathing Space meditation provides a way to step out of autopilot mode and anxiety, and reconnect with what is: right here,

right now. It also embraces a deep knowing that every moment – good or bad – passes at last. This is a very brief meditation (a few minutes will suffice), which can be done in any place: standing, sitting, kneeling, jogging, lying down, and so on.

1 Imagine the shape of an hourglass: it starts wide, then becomes narrow, and eventually widens out again.

2 **"Awareness of what is"**: bring yourself into the present moment. Gently close your eyes and ask yourself the following:

- What thoughts are arising in my mind right now?

- What feelings am I aware of right now?

- What sensations are present in my body at this moment?

Acknowledge everything you observe – even what is unwanted.

3 **"Focusing in"**: redirect your full awareness to the sensation of your breathing. Focus on each in-breath and out-breath coming and going. Your breath could be seen as your anchor, helping you to stay in touch with the "now". Take about ten mindful breaths.

4 **"Expanding awareness"**: now expand your sense of awareness and integrate awareness of your body as a whole. Perhaps imagine the circumference of your body, and sense the inhalation and exhalation from every body cell.

THE MOUNTAIN MEDITATION/ VISUALIZATION

FOR ALL WHO NEED TO RECONNECT TO THEIR INNER STRENGTH

1 Visualize the most beautiful mountain you have ever been on, or know from a picture, or can imagine. Notice its overall shape: the soaring peak, the base rooted in the rock of the Earth's crust and the sloping sides. Appreciate the fact that it is massive, unmoving, and preciously wonderful.

2 Now try and bring the mountain into your own body – your head becomes the towering peak; your shoulders and arms, the slopes of the mountain; your buttocks and legs, the solid base rooted to your cushion on the floor or to your chair. For this practice you become the breathing mountain, steadfast in your stillness – a centred, rooted, motionless presence.

3 Visualize the mountain, and all that lives on and around it, on a beautiful spring day. The sky is blue, the sun is shining, blossom is appearing on the branches of the trees. The mountain just sits, being itself and observing the world and how it changes.

4 Now imagine the same mountain on a rainy, thundery summer night. The environment has changed: everything is in full bloom, and luscious green trees and bushes are blown here and there by the strong wind. There is thunder and lightning in the air and nature feels distressed, and yet the mountain abides, watches, and remains as strong as it has always been.

5 At last see your mountain on a calm winter's day. It is snowing, nature is covered by a white blanket, and stillness is everywhere. As the daylight and darkness follow each

other, the mountain is purely being itself. It remains still as the seasons flow into one another. Its calmness is permanent and endures all change.

THE LAKE MEDITATION/ VISUALIZATION
FOR STRENGTH AND GROUNDEDNESS

1 Imagine sitting on a bench looking out at a beautiful lake. Sometimes its colour appears blue, at other times turquoise. The lake and you are surrounded by most beautiful, mighty mountains. Some are so high that you can see snow surrounding their lofty peaks.

2 You are looking at the lake, and the water seems calm and still. Occasionally a bird flies down to pick up an insect from the surface of the lake. At other times a trout or perch jumps up from the depths to catch a fluttering insect from the surface. You can see a mother duck with her ducklings swimming towards you, maybe hoping that you will feed them some breadcrumbs. In the distance are a couple of swans, majestic creatures in the process of cleaning their lovely white coats. The meadows around the lake are in full bloom: luscious green grass, meadow flowers in purple, yellow, pink, and white. There are some bushes and tall, ancient trees too. The sky is a heavenly blue, with just a few scattered clouds, and the sun is warming all creatures great and small. You can see butterflies, busy bees, and other insects, and birds in the air. Deep down in the lake there is another world: calm, with colours more muted but still beautiful, and peace abides.

3 Suddenly a storm starts to rise up. The sky begins to get heavy with dark-grey clouds. Soon rain is pouring down; the trees are bending from the force of the wind. The surface of the lake now appears a dark grey-blue, and big waves are chopping at the surface. Deep down, however, the lake hardly murmurs – stillness and peace still abide.

4 Apply this visualization to your own life. Imagine that even when all is topsy-turvy around you and you can barely cope, deep down there is this calm place that you have created through the practice of mindfulness, and you can return to it in your mind whenever you feel the need.

Mindful movement

These exercises are intended to show you that almost anybody can move their body – or at least parts of it. Your body needs, and delights, in movement. It is, however, really important that you only engage in those movements that you feel comfortable with. You can take it really slowly, and several of the exercises can be done either standing or sitting.

I will take you through a few "treasures of mini-movements" and, should you develop an appetite for it, you may want to start practising yoga, qigong, t'ai chi, or Pilates to take this journey further. Our bodies yearn for motion and, even if we are not altogether well or healthy in one or a few areas, doing these simple movements may prove to you that there's lot more right than is wrong with you.

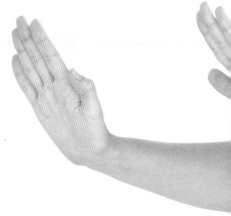

THE MOUNTAIN POSE

THE STANDING POSITION THAT STARTS MOST MOVEMENT PRACTICES (IT MAY ALSO BE DONE SITTING, BY THOSE WHO ARE UNABLE TO STAND)

This exercise strengthens you and improves your posture – and all this is achieved without really moving at all!

1 Begin by standing with the feet hip-width apart (arms by your side, palms facing in, gently touching the thighs).

2 Take a few breaths and get in touch with your breathing. When you are exhaling, contract the pelvic-floor muscles and lift them up until you feel a squeeze at the base of your buttocks – a physical sensation as if your sitting bones are coming closer. This action supports the spine from below. Continue to breathe evenly with the next exhalation, drawing the abdominals to the spine and at the same time lengthening the spine upwards.

3 Stand tall, with the spine erect and the head lifted. Breathe in deeply and widely into the lungs, creating with each in-breath a sense of space in the whole chest area. With the exhalation, roll the shoulders up, back, and down, releasing any tension there might be in the upper back.

4 Stand and feel, with each in-breath, the entire spine lifting upwards; and with each out-breath gently draw the navel to the spine, feeling the support that you are giving the lower back.

5 Shift your weight first into the right leg, noticing how the empty left leg feels, and then into the left leg. Really notice the focus you require in order to do that. Before you do the next exercise, return to the opening stance.

STRENGTHENING AND ENERGIZING ARMS AND WRISTS

1 Move your arms forward and up until they are parallel to the floor with palms facing down. Keep standing in the Mountain Pose (see pages 152–3) and sense your arms, while mindfully breathing in and out.

2 Now start gently rotating your wrists in one direction five times, followed by the opposite direction five times.

3 Gently become aware of any sensations in your arms, wrists, and your whole body. What is present: warmth, tingling, the muscles working hard to keep the weight of your arms up?

4 Now slowly permit your arms to return to the original position.

5 Breathe and stand in the Mountain Pose again, noticing any changes in your entire body. Are you breathing faster, deeper? Do you feel hotter? Do you feel more alive?

SHOULDER ROLLS

1 Start by standing or sitting in the Mountain Pose (see pages 152–3) and gently fold your arms at the elbows, so that you can place your hands, with the fingers slightly stretched, on your shoulders.

2 Breathe in and, with every out-breath, rotate your folded arms backwards. This releases tension in the shoulders and helps to increase their movement ability. Keep moving gently until you feel a sense of release.

NECK RELEASER

1 Keeping your chin parallel to the floor, breathe in and, on the out-breath, slowly and gently move your head towards the right shoulder, with the chin always parallel to the floor.

2 Reach the point where the stretch comes to a natural end. The breath will take you to the endpoint, which might extend naturally after a few times. Never use force. Then breathe in again and move your head back towards the starting point in the middle and, on the out-breath, move the head towards the left shoulder.

3 Continue to do these gentle moves and stretches several times in each direction.

4 Complete the Neck Releaser practice with your head in the middle, and come back into the Mountain Pose (see pages 152–3). Once again, feel deeply into your body and sense as best you can any subtle changes, such as temperature changes, tingling, and so on.

GENTLE CHEST OPENER

1 Roll up a bath towel and place it lengthways on a blanket or yoga mat. Sit with your buttocks on one end of the towel and then, supporting yourself with your arms, lower your spine over the rolled-up towel. Make sure that you are resting on the entire towel, from the tailbone to the top of your head.

2 Your arms should be by your side: they can either be close to the body, touching the outer edge of the mat, or even further up, in a T-shape. Your legs can be bent or stretched; you can have a rolled-up blanket under your knees to support the back of your legs. The legs are relaxed and fall open. If your head tilts backwards and your neck feels tight, place a pillow under your head. You are now opening your chest, and this can enhance your breathing. It will also help you to gently and compassionately reverse the close-down posture that often accompanies low mood. Stay in this position for 5–15 minutes.

3 To finish, roll over onto your side, then move the towel away. Roll over onto your back again, and feel the sensations in your back and chest.

SPINAL ROTATION

1 Lie on your back, with your legs and feet as for the Gentle Chest Opener (see pages 160–1), but this time stretch your arms to the sides into a V-shape, or even further up, to shoulder level, into a T-shape.

2 Inhale and exhale, then slowly lower your knees to the right. The buttocks should follow; the movement continues through your spine (like a corkscrew). Towards the end of the movement, turn your head to the left. Hold the position, inhale, and return to centre on the out-breath. Inhale in the centre position, exhale, then repeat on

the other side. Remember: move your body with the exhalation, and hold it with the inhalation.

3 Repeat three times on each side. On the last repetition, if you feel comfortable, hold for four to six breaths, and sink deeper into the position with each exhalation.

4 Now bend your legs, one after the other, into your chest and gently hold them, but avoid pulling them right into your chest. Keep your spine long as you move each vertebra to the floor, and avoid hunching up the shoulders. If you struggle to hug your legs, hold them behind the knees.

Stretching exercises

For those of you who feel able, here are a few stretches that you might wish to add to your mindful-movement practice. You can do these exercises at home or on holiday – there is no need to join a gym or buy special equipment. Your body loves to move, so give it this space for letting go.

All the movements, apart from the Cat Stretch (and its variations), can be done sitting down. So even if your mobility is limited, experiment with befriending your body again. Always "check in" for pain, as this is the body's way to let you know when to stop or not go any further. Only do those exercises that feel comfortable and that do not induce fear.

THE CAT STRETCH

FOR RELEASING TENSION IN THE BACK, SPINE, SHOULDERS, AND NECK (WATCH ANY CAT AND YOU WILL UNDERSTAND)

1 Using your mat and starting on your hands and knees, form a box position with the frame of your body, by placing your wrists directly underneath your shoulders, and your knees directly underneath your hips. If your wrists are weak, try rolling up the edge of a yoga mat or towel and placing your hands on it. To protect your knees, place a small cushion or folded towel under them.

2 Now lengthen your entire spine, from the top of your head to the tailbone. As you inhale, feel your abdomen move away from the spine; as you exhale, draw in your stomach muscles/navel towards the spine. Repeat this three more times and, with each exhalation, draw your abdomen/navel more towards the spine.

ANGRY CAT

1 From the Cat position (see page 166), draw your navel towards the spine, tucking your tailbone under and at the same time moving your chin in towards the chest. You are now rounding the spine, vertebra by vertebra, into a concave C-shape as you bring the pubic bone and the forehead closer to one another. It is as if you are balancing your body on top of a large beach ball.

SLEEPY CAT JUST WAKING UP

This is a great exercise for mobility of the spine, but if you have a lower-back problem and/or neck issues, start with a small movement and slowly increase your range of movement.

1 Begin to reverse the movement of the Angry Cat while exhaling. As you are releasing the abdomen slowly and in a controlled manner towards the floor, lengthen your spine into a neutral position.

2 Inhale, continuing the move, lifting your chest and breastbone forward and up and looking up. Keep your arms strong and your shoulder blades back and down.

3 Repeat this as many times as you did the previous stretch. Keep your navel pulled in towards your spine throughout the entire movement, to protect your lower back; do not bend your arms; keep your shoulder blades in the middle of your back as you round it into the C-shape, and let them slide down in the reverse C-shape.

THE LION POSE
FOR HELPING YOU FEEL POWERFUL AND IN CONTROL

Do this exercise when you need to boost your confidence. It is a great stretch for the tongue, many muscles in the face, the throat muscles, and to reduce tension in the chest. You can actually use it to let go of all tension, because relaxing the facial muscles has a positive effect on the whole body. You may even giggle or laugh, which is the best antidote to anger and stress.

1 Begin by sitting on a chair or kneeling on the floor with a cushion between your legs. Draw your navel towards your spine (this helps to support the lower back) and at the same time lengthen your spine, vertebra by vertebra, towards the ceiling. Inhale and allow your chest to expand, and on the out-breath roll your shoulders back and down (supporting the chest to stay open).

Lengthen your crown (the top of your head) towards the ceiling, with your palms resting on your thighs, facing down, and your elbows bent.

2 Now slide your palms towards your knees, gently hinging forward from your hips, but keeping your arms straight. Stop this movement when your palms cup your knees.

3 Press your palms against your knees and spread your fingers wide. Inhale deeply through your nose, and exhale while opening your mouth wide, without bringing any

tension to your jaw, stretching the tip of your tongue towards the chin as if you wanted to touch it, raising your eyebrows, rolling your eyes back, and looking to the point between your eyebrows. Breathe out through your mouth with the sound "Ha!" – similar to the roar of a lion – and then relax the facial muscles. Avoid bending your arms when you are "roaring"; keep your shoulder blades down in the mid-back and avoid any tension in your jaw. If it helps, you can try looking to the tip of your nose.

4 Repeat the movement sequence two more times, then return to your starting position.

PALM PRESS

FOR ACTIVATING THE PELVIC-FLOOR MUSCLES, BACK MUSCLES, AND HELPING TO LENGTHEN THE SPINE

1 Sit on a chair. Place your feet flat on the floor in parallel, with your hips and knees at a 90-degree angle and your palms resting on your thighs, pointing towards your knees. Inhale and, when you are exhaling, draw your navel to your spine.

2 Press your palms down onto your thighs. This will help to activate your pelvic-floor muscles and supports you in lengthening your spine towards the ceiling. Do this three to six times. Keep your shoulders relaxed and in the mid-back; avoid hunching them up, and apply equal pressure on your palms.

A GENTLE SELF-MASSAGE

FOR ENERGIZING THE BONE MARROW AND WAKING UP EVERY CELL OF YOUR BODY

When I lived in China my qigong master taught me the following practice. It can also be done while you are sitting down.

1 Take up the Mountain Pose (see pages 152–3), but bend your knees a little more. Try as best you can to stay loose and relaxed.

2 Lift your right hand and begin tapping your left hand and arm very gently. Starting at your fingers, slowly move up your arm, tapping softly all the way up and around. Take time to do this mindfully and do not leave out

any area, even tapping gently under the armpits to stimulate the glands, and on the shoulders as far down as you can reach; then gently do the exercise on the opposite side with the opposite arm.

3 When you have tapped both arms and hands lightly, continue by tapping the crown of your head. For this you can best use the tips of your fingers,

and both hands simultaneously, as if raindrops were falling on your head.

4 Then gently massage the face, again with the tips of your fingers. Massage the forehead and temples; around the eyes, nose, and sinus areas; the lips and around the lips; the chin and throat.

5 Now pull and massage your earlobes, first very gently, and then squeeze them between your forefingers and thumbs with a bit more vigour.

6 Continue the massage by tapping with both hands on your chest, abdomen, hips, and buttocks.

7 Then continue by tapping the right leg, and finish off with the left leg. You will now have gone round your body in a full circle.

8 If it feels right, gently swing your body from left to right a few times, with your arms dangling at your sides; and then from right to left a few times. Then return to stillness and the Mountain Pose. Once again the invitation is to feel deeply within your body and sense anything that you become aware of. Notice your breathing, your skin, temperature sensations, and anything else that arises.

THE ESSENTIAL MEDITATIONS

Walking exercises

Below is a saying of the Navajo people. Visualize inwardly whatever pictures your mind may create when contemplating this poem. Feel the beauty of life surrounding you before you take your first step of the walking exercises that follow.

I will be happy forever
Nothing will hinder me
I walk with beauty before me
I walk with beauty behind me
I walk with beauty below me
I walk with beauty around me
My words will be beautiful.

A MINDFUL WALK

When we walk mindfully we have the intention of getting from A to B, but have decided to do so with awareness, rather than using the time for planning or worrying.

1 Set your intention to really be present as soon as you start walking, and to focus on everything you sense as your feet touch different types of surfaces.

2 Take in anything that your eyes behold, however fleetingly, while also listening with awareness to the sounds that accompany you on your way – possibly even the air that touches your face and hands: ask yourself, does it feel warm or cold, moist or dry?

3 This exercise finishes when you reach your destination.

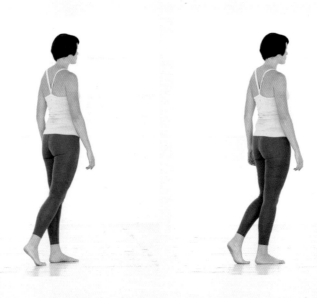

JUST WALKING

An alternative to the exercise above is a walking meditation. In this exercise you are not attempting to arrive anywhere. All you are intending to do is bring awareness to the action of walking by focusing on your movement from one end of the room to the other or from one end of your garden to the other. It means simply walking *and* knowing that you are walking.

You may notice that "simply walking" is not as easy as it sounds. Whenever you slow down and do something as if for the first time, it seems to be much more complex and challenging than you thought. Seeing toddlers learning to walk gives you an inkling of how difficult it is. They end up with a lot of bruises and frustrated efforts before they can do it properly. How wonderful that they don't give up easily!

1 Find a space that is safe for walking back and forth again on (you may want to try this with bare feet if you are indoors and know your "walking terrain"). All you require is a space that is about ten steps long in each direction. You may feel more relaxed if you select an area where you are not going to be observed by others.

2 Start by standing upright, and first shift your weight onto one leg while "peeling off" the floor the heel of the opposite foot. Walking meditation involves deliberately attending to the action of walking itself, and focusing initially on the sensations in your feet. The whole process may feel a little unsteady at the outset, but attempt as best you can to shift the lifted foot forwards and to gently place it down. You have just done one single step.

3 Feel into your body as you walk, noticing where the weight has shifted from and to. Feel the sensations in both of your feet: the one that is mainly carrying you now (the supporting

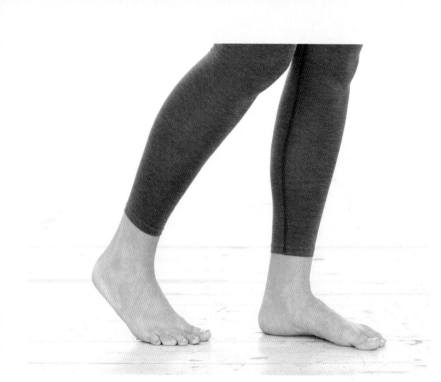

foot), and the other one, which may seem to have an "emptier" feel to it.

4 Repeat the same action with the other foot. You will become aware that when you placed one foot down, the heel of the other foot had already started to peel itself off the floor.

5 Move your second foot forward and place it down as well. Again the other foot will have been ready for this and will have started peeling the heel off the floor.

The slower you walk, the more aware you will become of the fundamental minutiae of walking: the lifting, shifting, and placing; the weight moving from right to left, left to right; and so on. It may occur to you what an incredible creation the human body is, and how wonderfully the body and the mind work together. When the mind wanders away from walking – as it undoubtedly will from time to time – stop for a moment and reconnect to the intention of this exercise.

You need not look around at your surroundings; just focus your eyes in front of you and avoid looking at your feet. The aim is to observe how your mind and body come together and deliver a step. Just feeling how this unfolds – that is all there is to it. It is enough just to be with each step, moment by moment.

You can practise "simply walking" anywhere: either slowly, so that one step might take "a lifetime", or at a more natural pace. You can even try it after some exercises in which you were moving more quickly. Then perhaps you can experiment with mindful rushing!

Sooner or later you will probably observe the critical mind rearing up, getting impatient with this whole practice: it might argue that you are wasting time, behaving like an imbecile. This is the point when you need to remind yourself that you are exercising your "muscle of mindfulness". Just like somebody who is training for a marathon or for skiing, you are engaging in a muscle-strengthening exercise.

Writing practice

I highly recommend that you obtain a journal for your mindfulness practice. This is meant solely for you to read (and to write in). It will help you to consider your response to each and every exercise.

You will notice how different each moment – even of the same exercise – can be. It depends on your daily mood, the time of the day, the place where you practise, and/or personal preferences.

After a month or so you will perhaps have an idea of which exercises suit you best. Sometimes, however, it is really helpful to try again an exercise that you felt less connected to. Everything changes, and thus a dislike can at times become a favourite. There is also some point in persevering with something that appears to be challenging. The exercises are like life itself: often, breaking though the

resistance they offer can open up a whole new world for you.

Below: *Create a mindfulness journal in which you can record your experiences and chart your practice.*

A SHORT STORY
FINDING YOUR WAY BACK TO YOUR BODY

I frequently run mindfulness workshops and try to combine a number of different mindfulness approaches in every session. Sue had been attending Wednesday-evening sessions for a while. I noticed that whenever I suggested mindful movement, she chose a sound or viewing exercise instead. One day I really sensed that her body was crying out for movement. As she had had a hip replacement and had a sore ankle, she felt her usual resistance. So I suggested to everyone that we would sit in a circle (because standing would have excluded her) and picked only exercises that she was able to follow, such as the Mountain Pose (see pages 152–3, seated option), neck, arm, and wrist exercises, the Lion Pose (see pages 170–1), and finally the Gentle Self-Massage I had learned from my qigong master (see pages 174–7).

Sue participated well, and seemed to become increasingly alert and at ease. When we finished she clapped her hands and was full of laughter, which soon changed to bitter tears. She later explained, "I realized that for the last twenty years I had given up on my body. It was fat, sick, and useless – and this 'mantra' I repeated to myself every time I saw myself in a mirror or shop window. Today I realized this is not so. I must try my best not to give myself a hard time for the years I missed out on enjoying my body. But now I know that there is a hell of a lot my body can still do. I am so grateful for seeing this at last."

188

Yoga exercises

In this section we will explore some simple movement practices, mostly from the yoga tradition. You will be able to experiment with gentle exercises that intend to get you back in touch with your physical awareness. Indeed, they may help you to see that there is more right than wrong with you!

THE MOUNTAIN POSE/STANDING POSITION
(WITH ARMS UP)

Benefits: Strengthens the legs, improves posture.

Position: Stand with your feet hip-width apart (*note: the hip sockets are set in from the hip bones by approximately 4–6cm (1½–2½in); hip-width apart means that the feet are within the frame of the pelvis – we are not referring to the outer hip measurements, when you buy some trousers*), your arms by your side, and your *palms facing in*, gently touching the thighs. Take a few breaths to become aware of your breathing.

Movement:

1 When you are exhaling, contract the pelvic-floor muscles and lift them up, until you feel a squeeze at the base of your buttocks – a physical sensation as if your sitting bones are coming closer. This action supports the spine from below.

2 Continue to breathe evenly, and with the next exhalation draw the abdominals towards the spine and at the same time lengthen the spine upwards. Standing tall, with the spine erect and the head lifted, breathe deep and wide into the lungs, creating with each in-breath a sense of space in the entire chest area.

3 With the exhalation, roll the shoulders up, back, and down, releasing any tension from the upper back.

4 Standing here, with each in-breath, feel the uplift in your entire spine; and, with each out-breath, as you gently draw your navel to your spine, feel the support you are giving your lower back.

Repeat: Three times.

The following is a progression of the Mountain Pose:

Movement:

1 Exhaling, stretch your arms down and, with the next inhalation, lift your arms out to the side and up towards the ceiling. Move slowly and continue lifting your arms overhead until the palms of your hands are facing each other. The arms should be in a V-shape, or shoulder-width apart and slightly closer together, or by the sides of the ears with your palms touching each other.

2 With every exhalation, roll the shoulders back and down, and with every inhalation try to stretch the arms a little bit more. When you can't move any further, hold the position for three to five deep breaths.

3 To return, lengthen the spine, turn the palms outwards so that the backs of the palms are touching each other, and with an exhalation start to move the arms out to the side and back down. Move slowly, until you are back in your starting position.

Repeat: Three times.

COMPLETE BREATH/ AWAKENING OR ENERGIZING BREATH

Benefits: Helps you to breathe more fully; awakens and energizes you to face the day with confidence and calm.

Position: Mountain Pose (see pages 152–3), with spine lengthened upwards, and your legs and feet hip-width apart. Your arms are by your side, with your *palms turned out*, so the thumbs face to the sides and the palms face the front.

Alternative: This can also be done sitting on a chair or on the floor.

Movement:

1 Inhale and sweep your arms slowly up and overhead, until your hands meet above your head and your palms touch.

2 Exhale slowly as you lower your arms back down to your sides, moving slowly in time with your breathing. See if you can deepen and lengthen your breathing and try to feel the pause after each breath. This way of breathing will help you to feel awake and energized and, at the same time, calm and centred.

Repeat: Five to eight times.

THE ESSENTIAL MEDITATIONS

THE STANDING STRETCH/STARFISH

Benefits: This pose strengthens the legs, back, shoulders, and arms. It gives you a feeling of being centred, and of energy and confidence radiating from the navel region and spine into your arms and fingertips.

Position: Mountain Pose (see pages 152–3), with your *palms at your sides*, facing/touching the outer seams of your thighs, fingers pointing down.

Movement:

1 Step your feet apart by moving the toes, then the heels, until they are about 50cm (20in) apart, with the *feet in parallel*. Move your pelvic floor in and up, and lengthen your spine upwards. Breathe and hold the position until you feel stable.

2 Inhaling, lift your arms out to the side and then up to shoulder height (you are now forming a T-shape with your arms), with your *palms facing down* and parallel to the floor. Keep lengthening your spine upwards, out of your pelvis, and squeeze your sitting bones together (pelvic-floor lift) to pull your tailbone down. Consciously relax the shoulders as you extend your arms and fingertips out to the sides.

3 Hold for three to five breaths.

Tips:

- Anchor your feet, using your heels and your big toe and little toe, so that you are firmly grounded.

- Bend your elbows a little, to avoid tension in your upper back.

THE POWERFUL GODDESS

Benefits: Firms the legs and thighs, improves your balance, brings awareness to the physical relationship between the pelvis and the upper body, and is a good tension-releaser/confidence-builder.

Position: You are standing in the Starfish position (see pages 194–5): with your *feet/toes turned out*, pointing to the corners of your mat. Your knees are in line with your toes. Your arms are straight and lifted to the side, with your *palms facing up*. Relax your shoulders back and down.

Movement:

1 Exhaling, squat down, bending your knees and tracking them to make sure they are directly over your feet. As you bend your legs, keep your spine straight, as if you are moving it between two magnets that are pulling the two ends of your spine further apart. At the same time, and still exhaling, bend your elbows at a 90-degree angle, spread your fingers wide – *palms now facing the front* – and exhale with a "Ha!" sound.

2 Breathe in and return to your starting position.

Repeat: Five to eight times, trying to squat a little bit deeper each time.

Tips:

- Ensure that your feet are turned out (in the "second position" in ballet) and your palms are facing up.
- Keep your abdominals drawn in and your back elongated.
- Track your knee/foot alignment to protect your knees.
- Try to press your knees open as you squat and squeeze your buttocks.

WARRIOR I

Benefits: Strengthens the feet, legs, and hips, and improves balance; also works your shoulders and back. The lifting of the arms overhead can give you a feeling of joy – like a victorious athlete or football player throwing his/her arms up to celebrate a win.

Position: Mountain Pose (see pages 152–3), *standing at the front of your mat*, with arms by the sides of your body.

Movement:

1 Exhale and, stepping back with your right foot and bending your left leg at the knee, come into a high lunge position. Your feet and hips point forward, and your back leg is straight, with the heel placed on the floor. Firmly ground yourself onto the back foot, but avoid collapsing into the inner arch of the foot. Your left knee is bent above the left ankle. Take a few breaths to find your balance.

2 Inhale and raise both arms slowly forwards and up, until they are close to your ears, parallel to each other, *palms facing each other*. Look ahead and hold for three to five breaths. Keep your shoulders relaxed, and avoid hunching them.

3 To get out of the pose, reverse the sequence as you lower your arms and step your right foot forward, parallel to your left.

Repeat: Do the same movement on the other side.

Tips:

- Only lift your arms when you have found your balance.
- Keep your body weight in your back leg.
- If parallel arms are difficult for you, ease off and make a V-shape with your arms.

STANDING SIDE-BEND/STANDING HALF-MOON

Benefits: Stretches the sides, opens the ribcage to deepen the breathing, works the waist, and improves balance.

Position: Mountain Pose (see pages 152–3), with the *palms flat* against the sides of the legs.

Movement:

1 Squeeze your buttocks, draw your abdominals in, and lengthen your spine, from your tailbone to the top of your head. Exhale and slowly bend to your right side, sliding the right palm down your thigh towards your right knee. Your left hand will slide up towards your left hip. Keep your head in line with your spine, looking forward. Hold for three deep breaths.

2 Exhale and then inhale; as your lungs and chest expand, slowly straighten your spine upwards again. Now your left palm will slide down and your right palm will slide up. Your head is the last thing to come up. Relax your

neck as you move your chin to your chest. Your spine stays straight.

Repeat: Do the same on the other side, then two more repeats on each side.

Tip:

● Avoid rotating your spine as you are bending. It helps to imagine that you are performing the move between two walls.

THE ROLL-DOWN/ TENSION RELEASE

Caution: Avoid this exercise if you have a disc-related ailment

Benefits: Increases spinal mobility, stretches the back muscles and hamstrings, works the abdominals.

Position: Mountain Pose (see pages 152–3), with *your arms by your side.*

Movement:

1 Lengthen your spine and, while breathing slowly and deeply, bring your chin to your chest and roll forward and down, as if rolling over a big ball. Your hands glide down your thighs and help you control the movement. Eventually you will hang forward and down from your hips, and your fingertips may touch the floor in front of you, with your buttocks in line with your heels.

2 Hold the position for several deep breaths and then slowly return. Exhale to squeeze your sitting bones together, draw your abdominals to your spine, and then – breathing in and out softly and deeply – straighten your spine as you roll up again, letting your head dangle, and your arms touch your legs, to support the movement. Bring your head up last, rolling your shoulders back and down. Stand tall.

Repeat: Three times.

Tips:

- Bend your knees if you have tight hamstrings.
- Draw your abdominals in as you move forward and down.
- Start with a half roll-down, stopping when your fingertips touch your thighs above your knees, then return to the upright position.
- Slowly increase your range of movement.

Alternative: Alternate knee to chest.

Position: Lie on your back with your feet on the floor, hip-width apart. Relax your lower back into the ground.

Movement:

1 Bring one leg into your chest, and hold and hug it there.

2 Lower the leg, then repeat on the other leg.

Repeat: Twice.

Tips:

- Avoid pulling your knee into your chest. Let it sink into the chest, and don't lift your hips or buttocks.

Depression- and anxiety-countering exercises

Depression and anxiety can overshadow the beauty and vividness of life around you. Practising mindfulness will get you closer to being more truly who you really are.

Although each of the formal and everyday practices is a balm for any wound, any problem, and any challenge, I have added on the pages that follow some suggestions for combating specific destructive emotions, including low moods, depression, anxiety, and fear.

Below: *Far away on the horizon, you may detect the shimmer of light that signals a new beginning.*

DEPRESSION/LOW-MOOD EXERCISE

1 Go to your meditation place and get into a comfortable and dignified position. Start the exercise by focusing on being really grounded – feeling your feet on the floor and your sitting bones on the chair, and then focusing on your breathing. Allow your breathing to continue as usual, and bring your awareness to it (acting as your anchor of attention).

2 When you sense a feeling of settling or calmness, say the following to your inner self: "Let me see you, Depression. Let me remember you in all your details." Now just keep breathing, and notice any information that arises in your awareness. It could be single words, sentences, feelings, sensations, colours, shapes, and so on.

3 As each piece of information arises, just notice it and let it pass by like a bird flying into the deep sky of your mind.

4 After a while, when the information starts to repeat itself or stops, return to focusing on your breath as your anchor of awareness, until you decide to end this meditation.

5 Now pick up your diary and note down all the information you gained throughn completing this exercise. Once you get going, you may remember more details about how depression manifests in your life, and your experience of it. Write these down too. As each person is different and unique, there may well be a number of aspects to it that have not been mentioned above.

DEPRESSION QUESTIONNAIRE
TRY THE FOLLOWING INTERVENTION:

An example of depressive thinking is: "I am a complete idiot, and nobody cares for me anyhow. I am lazy and no good, and even if I try, I will only fail again."

Identify whether or not you think this, or something similar. Identify the terms that you use to describe yourself in these situations, and really see what these negative evaluations do to you. Thoughts are not facts, but they can still hurt you if you believe in them.

● Do you tend to hold on to the same old thinking-spirals or patterns, fully knowing that they are neither true nor helpful? If so, see the thought as just a thought and try to let it pass, as if it were a balloon you can let go off (revisit the Sitting with Difficult Thoughts Meditation on pages 138–41), or a cloud in the sky that passes by.

- Are there any advantages or disadvantages of holding on to or changing this particular belief about yourself? What is the evidence that may support your belief? An advantage may be that it is easier to stay with the "devil you know". A disadvantage is continuing to be in mental pain and distress for longer and longer. As far as evidence goes, you might have to look near and far in order to find it.

- Can you design appropriate behavioural experiments to prove to yourself that you are not an idiot, or lazy, or a failure?

The fact that you are reading this book and experimenting with the meditations is definite proof that you represent none of these negative self-beliefs.

- How would you see yourself if you were not depressed? Perhaps you could ask friends, family, or other people who know you how they perceive you. Ask them what they like about you.

- If you have been depressed before, you can probably remember how depression gently lifted like a veil, and life looked more colourful again. So you could ask yourself how you see life when you are well, and how you see it when you are depressed? And how might this period of "unwellness" look three months on from now?

MINDFUL BREATHING FOR DEPRESSION

The breath is always there, and so you can access it without too much trouble.

1 Refer to the Mindful Breathing exercise on pages 134–5.

2 After doing the exercise, write down in your diary what came up, what you noticed, and how you are feeling after having done it.

3 In order to expand your awareness of breathing even further, you could see whether you notice your in-breath being cooler around your nostrils and your out-breath warmer. Focusing on such minute details really hones a deep awareness.

MINDFUL WALKING FOR DEPRESSION

In order to activate yourself – for the tiredness of depression has nothing to do with ordinary tiredness – you could try to experiment with fast mindful walking (see the exercise called A Mindful Walk on pages 180–1), as follows:

1 Find a spot where you can walk swiftly for about 20 steps. Stand in the Mountain Pose (see pages 152–3), with your legs hip-width apart, grounding yourself by sensing three points of contact (heel, big toe, and little toe). Let your shoulders hang loosely and your head and spine be upright. Let your gaze focus on one spot ahead, and avoid looking down at your feet.

2 Now start walking with vigour; your anchor of awareness is each step, which can be seen as a footprint on the ground. Also focus on your breathing, noticing its intensity rising with each step you have completed. Do this for about 20 minutes.

BRIEF BODY SCAN FOR DEPRESSION

1 Read the instructions for the Body Scan exercise (see pages 117–23).

2 This time you are invited to sweep *swiftly* through your body. This means paying perhaps less attention to each body part than in the detailed Body Scan, but instead breathing into each part and imagining a strong gust of wind sweeping through it. Perhaps have the intention to cleanse the whole system. You know how the wind often blows away lingering, unpleasant weather; so help your system free itself of "damp sadness". Just experiment a little. In this way the Body Scan becomes more active and invigorating, while at the same time you still attend to yourself with kindness and patience.

ANXIETY/FEAR: USEFUL PRACTICES

You now have a whole array of new ways to get unstuck from depression and, hopefully, to avoid a relapse. To overcome any general anxiety that you are experiencing, take time to look at some important insights below. You can use mindful interventions in a number of ways:

- Start each day with a short breathing practice (see pages 134–5, 136–7, and 192–3).

- Write a list of all the activities of the day that might make you feel anxious. Imagine coping with each individual action mindfully: taking an attentive, connected stance, grounding yourself with a breathing space, staying with each activity when it occurs, and dealing only with this particular challenge (not thinking ahead). "One at a time" could be your motto.

- Add compassion and patience to your daily list. Each experiment has a new beginning.

- Visualize yourself drinking in public; signing a cheque in a bank; paying a bill in a restaurant; eating soup in public; giving a talk in public, and drinking water during the speech. Even if your subconscious mind throws up a possibility of not getting it right, you could use humour to get through

THE ESSENTIAL MEDITATIONS

an awkward situation. If you spill your drink during your talk, you could say: "Fancy that – am I nervous or what?" Alternatively, you could just wipe off the spilt drink and continue as if nothing had happened. Because, in truth, is it really so terrible?

- Finish each day by remembering – even jotting down – all the little details you enjoyed, appreciated, and were satisfied with.

The second part of your plan should focus on remembering that, as mentioned earlier in this book, your thoughts are not solid, universal truths, so their power over you is no more than whatever you allow them to be. People or actions are only deemed "dangerous" if you apply an anxiety-provoking meaning to them. For example: "If my hands tremble when I sign the cheque, and the bank clerk notices it, I will look so stupid and will

feel like a total idiot." If you did not have this thought, you would either not experience the trembling at all or would simply accept that your hands sometimes tremble. Both of these options are versions of a rational and helpful mindset, which would not lead you to end up in a high-alert state. So remember: "Thoughts are not facts!'

So, when trying to drink water in public again, you may have thoughts such as "I will be so embarrassed if I spill this water or my hands are shaking." There may, however, be other thoughts that you could invite to your "thought party": "Even if I shake a little, who would even notice?"; or "If anyone did notice, they might feel empathy"; or even "Let them think what they like; at least I'm brave enough to do whatever suits me. I don't need anyone's approval."

CASE STUDY
MIRIAM, 42

Having lost my father when I was 30 and pursuing a stressful City-based job, it became apparent by my mid-thirties that I was not coping well.

I felt I was lurching between low mood and anxiety and, at times – if things got too much – panic attacks. I was introduced to meditation through the eight-week MBCT course and found that practising sitting meditation consistently allowed me a feeling of peace and space to address the issues that arose in my life. I realized that when I was experiencing a strong feeling or mood, I could sit with it, being more aware of the bodily sensations and tension that were fuelling it – in most situations this allowed me to step out of negative cycles and release stress.

Meditation has now become a very important part of my life. I try to practise daily, if only for ten minutes. It has opened me up to a greater awareness of my feelings, with less fear surrounding them and a sense of perspective, which helps me to realize that whatever is happening in that moment is not the whole story and will change and pass sooner or later.

I would definitely say that mindfulness has deeply affected my parenting, firstly in that it has allowed me to be more present and to let go of my agenda in favour of what is needed in the moment, to be more attentive, or at least aware when I'm not. Formal practice has offered me an oasis in the continual demands of parenting. Mindfulness also helps me to remain in the moment in some of the more mundane or repetitive aspects. But, above all, I think it's helped me to appreciate the impermanence of each stage and to truly appreciate and revel in small joys as they arise – to savour the special moments!

BREATHING EXERCISES FOR ANXIETY

One of the most common anxiety-provoked responses is hyperventilation. When you are breathing too fast you may experience a number of uncomfortable symptoms (a tingling face or hands, muscle tremors and cramps, dizziness and double/blurred vision, difficulty in breathing, tiredness, chest and stomach pains). So whatever position you are in when you notice shallow breathing, focus on the tip of your nose, feeling the airflow on the in- and the out-breath. You will probably notice cooler air entering your nose and warmer air leaving it. Simply focus on the in- and out flow in this way.

Another means of reducing "speedy breathing" is to inhale through your nose and exhale through your mouth, imagining holding a spoon with hot soup that you are trying to cool down and not spill. Do this five to ten times. See also the longer Mindful Breathing Exercise on pages 134–5.

Visualizations

Imagine being a mountain, remaining calm throughout a storm; or the sea, looking wild and ferocious on the surface, but deep down calm and still.

The first image may remind you of the Mountain Meditation/Visualization (see pages 146–7) and can help you feel grounded and empowered. And try the visualization below, to conjure up the latter image.

Below: The practice of using visualizations can have a profound effect on your life.

DEEP-BLUE SEA VISUALIZATION

1 Imagine sitting on a beach looking out at the beautiful sea. Sometimes its colour appears blue, at other times turquoise. The sea and you are surrounded by most beautiful palm trees and mangroves – luscious green all around you.

2 You are looking at the water, and the sea seems calm and still. Occasionally a white bird flies down to catch a fish swimming near the surface. At other times you may see dolphins jumping out of the water and pirouetting like a dancing star in the clear air. You may even see baby turtles, just hatched, hurling themselves into the sea for safety. In the distance you can see a big steamer and a few sailing boats. The sand on the beach glitters like golden and copper crystals. When you let it run through your toes, it tickles a little and warms your feet. There are a few coconut trees and their fruit is ripe and ready to be cut down. The sky is a heavenly blue, with just a few scattered clouds, and the sun is warming all creatures great and small. You can see little birds, green beetles, and other insects and can hear the sound of gentle waves. Deep down in the sea there is, however, another world. Calm, quiet, rich colours, a huge array of fish, octopi, crabs, plentiful shells – beauty and peace abide.

3 Suddenly a storm starts to rise up. The sky begins to get heavy with dark-grey clouds. The air feels laden with rain. Soon it is pouring down; the palm trees are bending because of the force of the wind. The surface of the sea now appears dark blue, and big waves are chopping towards the beach. Deep down, however, the sea hardly murmurs – stillness and peace still abide.

4 Apply this visualization to your own life. Imagine that even when all is topsy-turvy around you, and you can barely cope, deep down there is this place that you have created through the practice of mindfulness, and you can return to it in your mind, whenever you feel the need to.

EIGHT-SESSION MINDFULNESS COURSE TO OVERCOME DESTRUCTIVE EMOTIONS

Many eight-week mindfulness courses are now on offer. Some take place in a group setting, while others are offered on a one-to-one basis, either live or via Skype.

I'm inviting you to select a period of practice for yourself, in order to engage in the eight-session programme on the following pages. Should you find it useful, you may want to attend a course in person in the future.

Below: *Imagine this eight-session course as a bridge that will help you to "overcome" destructive emotions.*

Session 1: stepping out of autopilot

"Mindfulness is that space where you are in touch with life-experience and you are brightly aware."

BRYANT H MCGILL

The process of learning mindfulness is one in which we, as human beings, engage with the world around us in a completely new way. In order to achieve this, we must focus on awareness of the present moment, taking heed of both our mind and our heart as we do so. The goal is to reconnect to simply being alive and, at the same time, to let go of constantly "doing and striving".

Throughout the eight-session programme that follows we aim to enhance awareness, so that we can engage with and respond to situations through the power of choice, rather than relying on autonomous impulses.

Above: *Focus on awareness of the present moment.*

To achieve this we must work to change our focus, checking where our attention is and engaging our awareness in a way that allows us to shift it to our focus of choice.

It is important to remember that there is no right way of achieving this. Mindfulness is not a journey with the aim of progressing anywhere in particular; it's about taking in our surroundings and experiences and allowing ourselves to engage with them as we are. This is achieved through meditation practices that explore the virtues of patience, compassion, and opening the mind to life and its possibilities. Our body is the most important tool in achieving this, and only through discovery of inner stillness can we befriend it and begin to use and comprehend it to its full potential.

Second, we start engaging in everyday practices, so that anything we do becomes a mindful practice: brushing our teeth, washing the dishes, standing in a queue, and so on.

The importance of regular home practice

Our minds become accustomed to a particular way of approaching life, and it is through this that many of the habits we are now setting out to change have become second nature to us. Change can be achieved, however, through gentle and consistent persistence; new ways of feeling, thinking, perceiving, and behaving can arise.

Creating time for home practice is one of the more challenging aspects of this eight-session course. It is important to ease yourself into the process and to realise that it is only through regular practice that you will be able to feel the benefits of the practice and judge the effectiveness of mindfulness meditation for yourself. Only then will you be able to decide if you wish to use it going forward in your life. In order to achieve this, I would encourage you to record your experiences in a logbook or diary.

Dealing with difficulties

The intention of this process is to learn to live more in the present of each moment. Mindfulness encourages you to let go of judgement, allowing you to experience the present moment for what it is – and not what it could be. The ability to face what is unpleasant and challenging and, at times, maybe even learn to shorten this suffering can be a possible outcome.

Above: *If you invest time and effort through gentle and consistent practice, you will reap rewards.*

Patience and persistence

The road to change requires patience. Allowing yourself to invest time and effort will eventually allow you to reap rewards, both in body and in mind. These effects will take time to develop – much as a garden requires time to grow new seeds. Only with the right attention and adequate effort can they grow and truly flourish. Patience is required if the results are not immediately apparent; your effort will be rewarded sooner or later.

Focusing on minute changes

The overall goal of this course is to learn new ways to help you improve your well-being, while also being able to handle challenging moods and emotions with kindness. You begin this by concentrating on minute changes at first: combining feelings, thoughts, and bodily sensations (as in the Raisin Exercise opposite) in order to better determine your mood. This will allow you to focus on any noticeable changes and become more astute and aware.

Below: *Don't expect the results of your efforts to be immediately apparent. Patience is required.*

THE RAISIN EXERCISE

This exercise shows you how, in the moment, your attention is not always focused on the task at hand when you are eating. You therefore lose out on the vibrancy and richness of life, and all the wonderful experiences within it. It also teaches you how, by being aware of the moment and everything in it, you can begin to alter your own experiences and deepen your understanding of them.

1 Get hold of a few dried raisins, then sit down in your meditation place and put them in your palm. You may notice how they vary in size, structure, and colour.

2 Now pick up one of the raisins and press it between your thumb and forefinger. Is it dry or moist? Does it change its shape? Now sniff it, and determine whether you can actually smell anything; if so, what does this smell remind you of? Is it pleasant or unpleasant? Now lift the raisin near your ear and squish and rub it. Can you hear a sound? Let yourself be surprised by your sensations.

3 The time has come to receive the raisin into your mouth. What does your body have to do? How does it prepare itself? Watch the movements: tongue, jaw . . . And now let the raisin rest on your tongue, and see whether you detect any taste. If not, slowly begin to chew (if yes, do the same): notice

how the shape and texture of this little piece of food changes. What kind of taste explodes in your mouth? Is it what you expected? How long do you need to chew before the raisin is a soft pulp? Now prepare to swallow it, and notice once again what your body needs to do. Do you feel it landing in your stomach? What taste remains in your mouth? What do your teeth do now? Do you fancy another raisin? What was the whole journey like?

4 Now take a moment to write down your experiences in your diary.

Eating mindfully

After having practised the Raisin Exercise, you can now apply the same attitude to any food that you choose to eat. Even if you only apply it to the first few spoonfuls of soup, muesli, and so on, try to eat as if you had never eaten such fantastic food before – feel in touch with each step, and deeply enjoy the huge variety of groceries from which you can choose.

So, should you choose to eat some porridge mindfully, you can start by feeling the shape and surface of the bowl with one hand, and experience how the other hand guides the spoon to scoop up some lovely, steaming porridge. Now focus on the texture, and how it slides easily down your food pipe. Now for the taste: did you add water and milk, sugar and salt, as traditionally done in Scotland? Can you taste each of those ingredients? How about sprinkling a little cinnamon on top? It is a lovely addition and gives you a sense of warmth and homeliness.

The more you eat with this attitude, the slower you will eat and the sooner

Right: *Take pleasure in the art of living daily: prepare, cook, and eat with great awareness.*

you will feel full. It will also become much harder to eat food that is not actually good for your body. Fast foods, or dishes that contain too much fat or salt will lose their appeal. Give it a try and see for yourself.

Autopilot mode

When we are driving a car, many drivers enter what could be considered "autopilot" mode. In this state they become removed from their conscious actions, functioning on a basic level and falling "victim" to any negative arousal.

By raising awareness of our feelings, thoughts, and body experiences as a whole, we give ourselves greater freedom to respond.

In much the same way, we live our lives not entirely in the present moment. The sensation of being "far away" or detached can leave many of our day-to-day experiences feeling empty and unfulfilling. We tend to forget the good and beautiful moments and are more likely to "have our buttons pressed" by situations around us that we cannot control. By raising awareness of our feelings, thoughts, and body experiences as a whole, we give ourselves greater freedom to respond. This can lead to the ability to choose not to repeat "mental ruts" that may have caused problems in the past.

To begin with, we must focus our attention on different parts of the body. We use these as anchors for our awareness, and through this practice we can train ourselves to put awareness and attention in different places at will. The Body Scan exercise (see pages 117–23) allows this to occur, and assists us to awaken to each area of our physical being.

HOME PRACTICE FOR SESSION 1

- Do an ordinary activity mindfully every day.

- Write down an appointment with yourself for a time slot that you want to use for the Body Scan practice (see pages 117–23), and practise it most days. Try it sitting upright or lying down. Should you fall asleep, be compassionate towards yourself. Most people do not sleep enough in the 21st century.

- Eat or drink something mindfully every day, just as you did in the Raisin Exercise.

HOME-PRACTICE RECORD FORM

You can record your comments on this form each time you practise and make a note of anything that comes up in your homework, so that you can compare and contrast how each day and each practice is a new experience.

DAY/DATE	PRACTICE

COMMENTS

Session 2: dealing with barriers

"The present is the only time that any of us have to be alive – to know anything – to perceive – to learn – to act – to chance – to hear."

JON KABAT-ZINN, *FULL CATASTROPHE LIVING*

Throughout this process we invite ourselves to take an interest in how our minds react to certain exercises. It is through powerful mental activities that we can lose the ability to live in the moment – automatic tendencies judge the experience before we have actually lived it. This can lead to us feeling deprived and empty in our day-to-day lives, even feeling that something in our experience is not right. These judgements can in turn lead to sequences of self-doubt, and can cause us to blame ourselves for feeling this. Often these thoughts will take us down familiar paths in our mind (anger, depression, fear, and so on). Through this we lose touch with the moment, and thus with the freedom in our mind to make choices.

In order to break this cycle we must acknowledge the reality of the situation around us. We must see it for what it is, and cast aside automatic tendencies. The Body Scan exercise (see pages 117–23) provides ample opportunity to practise a new way of thinking, and opens up the possibility of real change in the way you experience the moment – provided that you approach it with an open and willing mind.

Right: *Seemingly insurmountable barriers can be compounded by negative and restrictive thoughts. By recognizing our limiting beliefs we can reveal opportunities that were previously hidden from sight.*

Below are a few tips for the Body Scan exercise, which by now you have, hopefully, practised a number of times.

- Just do it! Go with the flow and give it a try; experience the Body Scan, regardless of what happens. Every experience is different and can yield unexpected outcomes.

Simply see these as aspects of your journey.

- Your mind may wander during the process. Simply note the thoughts as passing events, and let your mind move gently back to your body scan.

- Encourage yourself to practise. Do not allow yourself to see this as a test that can be "passed" or "failed". Let your mind be open and curious, and cast aside the notions of this being a competition. Trust the tens of thousands of research papers that claim this practice will have benefits for those who perform it.

- Approach the exercise with an open mind. Expectations will only serve to distract you. You must see the body scan as a process that is fluid, and one that should be allowed to develop naturally. The right conditions – along with regular and frequent practise – will in time bring about their own positive outcomes.

- Approach your experience with the mindset that each moment is just as it should be. Don't attempt to fight off unpleasant thoughts, feelings, or body sensations; this will only lead you away from your destination.

- By not forcing or expecting pleasant feelings, you encourage them to emerge of their own accord. When you stop resisting unpleasant feelings, you will find they begin to drift away on their own. When you stop trying to make something happen, you open your mind to fresh and unexpected experiences.

MINDFUL BREATHING EXERCISE

(FOR A LONGER VERSION, SEE PAGES 134–5)

1 Sit in a comfortable position. Allow your shoulders to drop, and keep your spine straight. Close your eyes, if this feels comfortable.

2 Focus on your body sensations. Focus on your sense of touch, contact, and pressure in your body, and feel where it makes contact with the floor or whatever surface you are sitting on. Spend a few moments engaging and exploring these sensations.

3 Feel each breath: the rise of your stomach as you breathe in, and the falling as you breathe out.

4 Remain focused on your breathing. Follow each breath for its full cycle: each in-breath and out-breath, for as long as it takes.

5 Allow your mind to focus on your breath. Should your focus wander, simply notice what caused it to drift, then allow yourself to focus again on the rise and fall of your stomach. Every time your mind wanders from your breath, your "job" is simply to bring it back. Being aware of your mind wandering is just as crucial as being aware of your breath.

6 Each breath has its own beginning and ending; let your body breathe itself. Notice that after each in- and out-breath there is a little pause.

HOME PRACTICE FOR SESSION 2

- Do an ordinary activity mindfully every day.

- In addition, practise ten minutes of Mindful Breathing (see pages 134–5 and 235) each day.

- Write down an appointment with yourself for a time slot that you want to use for the Body Scan practice (see pages 117–23), and practise it most days. Try it sitting upright or lying down. Should you fall asleep, be compassionate towards yourself. Most people do not sleep enough in the 21st century.

- Pleasant-event diary: fill in one pleasant event each day for a week on the form on pages 240–1.

HOME-PRACTICE RECORD FORM

You can record your comments on this form each time you practise and make a note of anything that comes up in your homework, so that you can compare and contrast how each day and each practice is a new experience.

DAY/DATE	PRACTICE

COMMENTS

PLEASANT-EVENT DIARY

	What was the nature of the pleasant event or experience?	Were you aware of the pleasant feelings *while* the event was happening?
Monday		
Tuesday		
Wednesday		
Thursday		
Friday		
Saturday		
Sunday		

How did your body feel, in detail, during this experience?	What moods, feelings, and thoughts accompanied this event?

Session 3: the breath

"Use the breath as an anchor to tether your attention to the present moment. Your thinking mind will drift here and there, depending on the currents and winds moving in the mind, until, at some point, the anchor line grows taut and brings you back."

JON KABAT-ZINN, *MINDFULNESS MEDITATION FOR EVERYDAY LIFE*

Bringing awareness to the breath

Focusing on this very moment – the here and now – is what allows us to use it as an anchor. It really does not matter where we are. This can change our perspective. It connects us with a wider awareness, and creates a broader outlook from which we can view situations.

How to sit when meditating

Sitting is a crucial part of this process. Allow yourself to be positioned in a fully erect and dignified posture. Your head, neck, and back should be aligned vertically – this acts as a physical reminder to an inner attitude of alertness and kindliness.

Practise either on a chair or on the floor. Should you choose a chair, ensure it is one with a straight back that enables you to place your feet flat on the floor. Should it be too tall, put a cushion under your feet. And try to give yourself the chance to sit away from the back of the chair, allowing your spine to support itself. You can assist this by putting a rolled-up towel in the hollow part of your lower spine.

Right: *When meditating, assume an upright posture, maintaining dignity and poise, much like the Buddha.*

If you choose to sit on the floor, do so with a firm support beneath you (a thick cushion, a *zafu* meditation cushion, or a pillow folded over twice should suffice). If you cross your legs, make sure your knees are not "hanging" unsupported in the air. Again, roll up small towels and support your knees in this way (creating a triangular base). Alternatively you can get a little bench to support the back part of your buttocks, then kneel on a well-cushioned mat.

Being mindful and aware

Young people tend to be more physical and in tune with their body than older people. As we mature, we begin to lose this physical awareness and slip into "autopilot" much more: we get lost in the past, are fearful about the future, and are rarely fully "awake". The more we practise mindfulness, the more we feel alert and in touch with what is actually going on in our lives. We move into present-moment awareness.

One key aspect of mindfulness is paying attention, on purpose and free of judgement. This allows us to see our body and mind in a new light, and lets us engage with the world in a more "present" manner". Most individual practices focus on one sense only, as an anchor of awareness.

Walking meditation

The practice of "Just Walking" (see pages 182–4) is a simple way to bring

awareness into your daily routine. It involves bringing your attention to the generic experience of walking. It means knowing that you are walking while you are walking – just this one thing. Mindfulness, however, is not all that simple (maybe you have observed this by now). While walking, we tend to get drawn into thinking, planning, wondering, ruminating, remembering, and thus we hardly ever "just go for a walk".

Above: *Mindful walking – or "just walking" – brings a heightened sense of awareness into your life.*

Walking meditation invites you to simply attend to the experience of walking itself. It involves the sensations in your feet, legs, and even your whole body, and focuses on these aspects while moving. Breathing can also become a part of this experience.

With the first step it is important to be fully aware as one foot makes contact with the ground, noticing how the weight shifts onto it, as the other foot lifts and moves ahead and is then placed down. Remember the importance of focusing as much as possible on this "shifting": the action of moving forward and placing. Your mind will wander, and this is to be expected. Keep your gaze fixed ahead and avoid looking at your feet. All you are doing is focusing on the sensations of walking.

When you engage in a walking meditation, your goal is not to get anywhere. Instead you want to feel each step, become a part of each step. To achieve this you must be as aware as possible. Of course your mind will try and do its own thing, and you need to accept this. Sometimes you will be able to "lasso it in" and stay with the sensations of each step; at other times you will suddenly wake up from imagining a conversation or a shopping list. Judgement may also arise at times, and may label your walking forward for ten steps or so and then

Above: *Bring awareness to the action of walking by focusing on the sensation of the earth beneath your feet as they make contact with the ground.*

back to your original starting point "a waste of time". Just trust that millions of meditators around the globe and over the centuries have engaged in this practice and got something out of it. See for yourself what it may offer you.

Mindful walking does not have a set location. Sometimes you will find it easiest to take it slowly; this allows you to engage intensely with each moment as it occurs. Normal walking pace is also acceptable. A quick pace won't allow you to be in each moment as deeply as you would be at slower speeds; however, you can simply shift your awareness to the whole of your body – even when rushing – so long as you remember to be mindful.

The mind craves something new. Walking is not new to our minds, because it occurs so often, as part of our daily routine; it can be exhausting, depressing, and monotonous at times. By bringing awareness to this mundane task we short-circuit the autopilot mode and make this simple experience more vivid. We engage with the world around us, and this task becomes much more enjoyable and interesting, while also leaving us calmer and less exhausted at the end.

In summary, walking opens the opportunity for mindfulness. Sometimes it's good to do this in isolation, as it allows you to engage fully in each moment, one step at a time, walking gently on the Earth, and allowing you to feel and enjoy exactly where you are.

When you engage in a walking meditation, your goal is not to get anywhere. Instead you want to feel each step, become a part of each step. To achieve this you must be as aware as possible.

It can be challenging to timetable slots to do the home practice that is part of this course. You need not decide yet whether you will continue your regular practice tomorrow or for the rest of your life. This can wait until you have completed the course. Only if you practise regularly will you be able to judge whether meditation is a skill that you want to continue in the future.

THE THREE-MINUTE BREATHING SPACE

This exercise can be done while standing or walking, sitting or lying, so in Session 3 you can do it while walking, as part of your walking meditation.

1 Awareness: Bring yourself into the present moment by adopting a dignified posture. You can stand, sit, or use any other pose. Gently close your eyes and ask: "What is my experience right now: in thoughts . . . feelings . . . and bodily sensations?" Stay with this for a few moments. Acknowledge the experience, even if it is unfulfilling.

2 Gathering: Now direct your full attention to your breathing: to each in-breath and out-breath as it comes and goes. Allow each breath just to unfold naturally. Don't change anything. Your breath could be seen as your anchor, helping you to stay in touch with the "now" and leading you into peacefulness.

3 Expanding: Now expand your field of awareness around your breath, so that it includes an awareness of your body as a whole. Perhaps mentally draw a line around your whole body. Feel your feet grounded fully. If you wish, visualize an image of strength and solidity – a mountain, a tall tree, and so on.

This sequence is rather like an hourglass in shape: wide focus, followed by narrow focus, followed by wide focus. The key skill in developing mindfulness is to maintain awareness in the moment. Nothing else.

HOME PRACTICE FOR SESSION 3

- Practise mindful movement: yoga, Pilates, t'ai chi, qigong, or mindful walking. Or follow one of the Essential Meditations (pages 106–219). The point of focusing on gentle movement is to provide a direct way to connect with your body. The body is a place where the emotions often get expressed beneath the surface, and without your awareness. Working with your body gives you a means to experience more of yourself. The movements activate the body and mind and reduce tiredness. (If you have back or other health difficulties, discuss with your GP or a personal trainer which exercises would be suitable for you.)

- On alternate days practise the Body Scan (see pages 117–23).

- At a different time practise ten minutes daily of Mindful Breathing (see pages 134–5 and 235) and make a record of your reactions.

- Engage in practice of the Three-Minute Breathing Space (see page 249) three times daily.

- Unpleasant-event diary: fill in one unpleasant event each day for one week on pages 254–5. Notice what thoughts, feelings, and body sensations were present at the time the event occurred. Record your observations as soon as possible afterwards.

HOME-PRACTICE RECORD FORM

You can record your comments on this form each time you practise and make a note of anything that comes up in your homework, so that you can compare and contrast how each day and each practice is a new experience.

DAY/DATE	PRACTICE

COMMENTS

UNPLEASANT EVENT DIARY

	What was the nature of the unpleasant event or experience?	Were you aware of the unpleasant feelings *while* the event was happening?
Monday		
Tuesday		
Wednesday		
Thursday		
Friday		
Saturday		
Sunday		

How did your body feel, in detail, during this experience?	What moods, feelings, and thoughts accompanied this event?

Session 4: staying present

"The key to transformation is to make friends with this moment. What form it takes doesn't matter. Say yes to it. Allow it. Be with it."
ECKHART TOLLE

Life can be difficult – nobody will deny this. However, it is *how* we handle challenging situations that affects whether we are in control, rather than events controlling us. Mindfulness teaches us how we can change from reacting habitually to responding wisely to a difficult life event.

We have a tendency to *react* to life's challenges in one of three ways:

- With *indifference*: by daydreaming, indulging in escapism or planning exciting things for the future. It is not wrong to switch off, but it rarely leads to any change in the cumbersome situation.

- With *attachment*: having an expectation that a good thing – such as delicious ice-cream – will always taste good or always be available; if not, it's the end of the world.

- With *aversion*: wanting to rid ourselves of a difficulty or avoiding it. If there are queues in the supermarket, switching from one queue to another is rarely the answer.

Each of these ways of *reacting* can cause even more problems. In this session we want to attempt to become more aware of our experience, so that

we can learn to *respond* mindfully, rather than *react* automatically.

When we practise mindfulness meditation regularly, we experience the struggles of the mind. These practices are like allegories of life, and the difficulties that we face when we are up and about also present themselves

Above: *The hub of the Buddhist Wheel of Life contains a pig, a snake, and a bird, who in turn represent the three poisons (or unwholesome mental states) of indifference, attachment, and aversion.*

when we are sitting on our meditation cushion. There could be impatience; apathy and boredom; and a type of clinging, when the meditation is "going really well" and we are on cloud nine.

Above: *Endeavour to let go of negative thinking.*

Negative automatic thoughts (NATs)

NATs can repeatedly push us into emotional despair and imbalance. You may have learned them in early childhood, by copying a significant adult for instance, or by believing things that others said about you. Of course there are many mental errors that the brain is capable of repeating. The most common ones are listed opposite:

- I feel like I don't agree with anyone else.

- I am a waste of time.

- Why can't I ever be successful?

- No one can truly understand me and my suffering.

- I am totally unreliable.

- I don't think I can do this any more.

- I wish I wasn't so pathetic.

- I can't sort out my life.

- I despise myself.

- Nothing ever feels like fun.

- I have had enough.

- What's wrong with me?

- I wish I was in another place or on another planet.

- My life's going nowhere and is a huge disappointment.

- I am completely worthless.

- I wish I could just disappear.

- I am a loser.

- I'm a failure.

- I will never make it.

- I feel so hopeless.

- My future is bleak.

- I am so bored with it all.

- It is just not worth it.

- I can't complete anything.

Perhaps seeing all these NATs gives you a little insight into the world of negative thinking. If you engage in just a few of the above thinking patterns, it will appear that your life is not worth a lot. You may also have noticed that many of the patterns of thinking are absolutist: all or nothing. They do not offer a grey area in between. Is this really possible? Have you ever seen any of your friends feeling quite as bad as you *think* you feel?

If several of these NATs are ongoing for more than a very short time, you should seek professional help.

Seeing what these thoughts achieve (or, rather, what they fail to achieve)

The more mindful and aware of these thinking errors you become, the less you will want to hold onto them. You can learn to understand that nobody is perfect, but also that you are not as bad as you think you are. There will be a kind of gentle "letting go" of negative thinking . . . and it will happen organically. Mindfulness's other side (the Ying to its Yang, in terms of the Chinese symbol of life) is compassion; the more you feed this kindly awareness, the less you will harshly criticize yourself.

Noticing how such thoughts affect you physically and emotionally

The first time you were invited to note the connection between negative thinking and body sensations and emotions was in Session 3, when you were asked to fill in the unpleasant-event diary (see pages 254–5). You are persistently recommended to look deeply into the connection between body, mind, and feeling. These negative thoughts don't just provoke more thoughts of the same ilk and negative reactions thereafter, but they can also acutely affect your emotional state and how you move, hold yourself physically, and interact with others.

SITTING WITH DIFFICULT THOUGHTS MEDITATION FOR LETTING GO OF NATs
(SEE PAGES 138–41 FOR AN EXTENDED VERSION)

This meditation is one in which you actually focus on arising thoughts. The approach is to actively watch thoughts as mental events, without allowing them to draw you into a funnel of negativity. You will attempt to let each thought arise and pass by, and likewise to allow sounds to enter your awareness and pass through it. All the while you remain in control. In this meditation look at your thoughts as if you're an external observer, seeing them for what they are: events of the mind, and not necessarily true, false, or important in any way. The invitation is to remain detached. Perhaps see each thought like a cloud or a balloon passing by. Note it and then let go of it.

1 Start this practice by focusing on your breath.

2 Refer to the Difficult Thoughts Meditation on pages 138–41.

3 The poem below gives you an idea of how you can learn to be free of such destructive thoughts, and this freedom evolves through the meditative practice.

4 Finish this practice by focusing on your breath.

Free

Grounded in the present,
I am free from the past,
Gently evolving changes
That I know are to last.
I check on my thoughts
And the future I see
Back to the present,
Once more I am free.
But I'm busy says the mind,
More thoughts there I find.
Watch them pass away,
Why let my mind spoil the
     enjoyment of today.

KAREN NEIL

HOME PRACTICE FOR SESSION 4

- Practise Mindful Walking (see pages 180–1) and/or walking meditation (see pages 244–7). Record your practice each day, and your reactions to it, on your record sheet, if you wish to.

- On alternate days practise Mindful Breathing (see pages 134–5).

- Practise the Three-Minute Breathing Space (see page 249) at least three times a day. Either practise it when you think of it, or connect it to three regular activities that you do, or to places you visit every day (for example, on waking up and/or going to bed; before eating; after washing your hands; on first sitting down in your car or on the bus, or at your desk).

HOME-PRACTICE RECORD FORM

You can record your comments on this form each time you practise and make a note of anything that comes up in your homework, so that you can compare and contrast how each day and each practice is a new experience.

DAY/DATE	PRACTICE

COMMENTS

Halfway review

This course is attempting to help you become proactive in improving your own health and mental well-being.

Sessions 1–4 have focused on the autopilot mode of your mind; you were introduced to coming back to the present moment and to developing attention skills (connecting to the breath, sound, and so on).

In the second half of the programme you will be introduced to cultivating a different relationship to your daily experiences.

Kindly think about the insights you may have gained so far, by focusing on the following questions:

- What am I learning through this process?

- How can I get the best out of the course?

Reread all the recommendations that have been made so far with focus and awareness!

Session 5:
"let it be" and accept

"Your joy is your sorrow unmasked and the selfsame well from which your laughter rises was oftentimes filled with your tears."

KAHLIL GIBRAN

When difficulties arise, a common and understandable response can be to stuff them down or to turn away from them. But this kind of resistance and denial require an enormous amount of effort and can often lead to even more discomfort. As an alternative to this, I want to

Below: *Bringing compassionate awareness to your problems and embracing discomfort brings change.*

introduce you to the possibility of accepting and handling adversity.

Initially, accepting something that hurts or burdens you can be a difficult prospect to engage in. However, you are not expected to resign yourself to your problems, but rather to bring

compassionate awareness to them. Getting closer to your discomfort and embracing it can cause it to change, or even disappear altogether.

The basic guideline in this practice is to become mindfully aware of whatever is most dominant in your moment-by-moment experience. So if your mind is being repeatedly drawn to a particular place, to particular thoughts, feelings, or bodily sensations, you should deliberately give gentle and friendly awareness to that place. That is the first step.

The second step is to notice, as best you can, how you are relating to whatever is arising in that place. Often you may relate to an arising thought, feeling, or bodily sensation in a non-accepting, reactive way. If you like it, you tend to hold onto it (attachment); if you do not like it, because it is painful, unpleasant, or uncomfortable, you tend to contract and push away,

Left: *Anchor your awareness in your bodily sensations and then use the breath to open to your feelings.*

out of fear, irritation, or annoyance. Each of these responses is the direct opposite of acceptance.

The easiest way to relax is, first, to stop trying to make things different. Accepting an experience means simply allowing space for whatever is going on, rather than trying to create some other state. Through acceptance we settle back into awareness of what is present. We "let it be" and simply notice and observe whatever is already present. This is the way to relate to experiences that have a strong pull on our attention.

For example, if you notice that your awareness keeps being pulled away from the breath (or any other focus of attention) to particular sensations in the body associated with physical discomfort, emotions, or feelings, the first step is to become mindfully aware of those physical sensations, and to deliberately move your focus of awareness to the part of the body where those sensations are strongest.

The breath is the best ally to do this – just as you practised in the Body Scan (see pages 117–23), you can take a gentle and friendly awareness to a particular part of the body by "breathing into" that part on the in-breath, and "breathing out" from it on the out-breath.

Accepting an experience means simply allowing space for whatever is going on.

Once your attention has moved to and is anchored in your bodily sensations, you could say to yourself, "It's okay. Whatever it is, it's okay. Let me feel it." Then try and use each out-breath to soften and open to the sensations that you become aware of.

Acceptance is *not* resignation – acceptance allows us, as a vital first step, to become fully aware of difficulties, and then (if appropriate) to *respond* in a skilful way, rather than to *react* habitually.

USING THE THREE-MINUTE BREATHING SPACE TO COPE WITH DIFFICULTIES

When you are feeling troubled by your thoughts or feelings, try using the Three-Minute Breathing Space (see page 249) as follows in order to cope.

1 *Awareness of the difficulty*

Acknowledging: Bring yourself into the present moment by deliberately adopting a dignified posture. Then ask, "What is happening to me right now?" Notice, acknowledge, and identify what it is. Put your experience into words; for instance, say in your mind: "There are feelings of rage/sadness . . . "

2 *Redirecting attention*

Gathering: Gently focus your full attention on your breathing. Experience each in-breath and out-breath as they follow one another. You may find that it helps to note

at the back of your mind: "Breathing in . . . Breathing out . . . ", or to count your breaths. The breath can function as an anchor to bring you into the present and to help you to be still and grounded.

3 *Expanding awareness*

Turning towards: Expand your awareness to your whole body and the space it takes up, as if your whole body is breathing. Perhaps draw a mental line around the circumference of your body. You could choose to breathe in and out of the difficulty, too.

Finally, visualize a symbol of strength, for example, the sea, the sun, a mountain, a big tree, a horse, and so on.

I am not encouraging you to try and resolve anything by "being with" these uncomfortable emotions, but instead ask only that you act like a detective, investigating the nature of the discomfort. By turning towards, rather than pushing against these thoughts, you may begin to notice a change in your perception.

"The Guest House" (see page 273), by the 13th-century mystic and Sufi poet Rumi, talks about the human condition and puts an unexpected slant on it.

The Guest House

....

This being human is a guest house.
Every morning a new arrival.
A joy, a depression, a meanness,
some momentary awareness comes
as an unexpected visitor.
Welcome and entertain them all!
Even if they're a crowd of sorrows,
who violently sweep your house
empty of its furniture.
Still, treat each guest honourably.
He may be clearing you out
for some new delight.
The dark thought, the shame,
the malice.
Meet them at the door laughing,
and invite them in.
Be grateful for whoever comes,
because each has been sent
as a guide from beyond.

RUMI (TRANSLATED BY COLEMAN BARKS WITH JOHN

MOYNE), *THE ESSENTIAL RUMI*

This poem invites you to see the human condition objectively. Every one of us is a guest house visited by both welcome and unwelcome guests, and none of them should be invited to stay for long. Even though you might rather never experience the negative ones, you will not be able to avoid them altogether. They are real and must be dealt with – like it or not. The good news is spelt out in stanza three: they "may be clearing you out for some new delight". And it's so true, isn't it? Often, after a painful experience, there is space for something new and exciting to come into your life.

EIGHT-SESSION MINDFULNESS COURSE TO OVERCOME DESTRUCTIVE EMOTIONS

SEEING YOUR PAST AS A MOVIE

If you try to bring up painful memories, you may discover just how hard it can be. The reason is that you probably spent a lot of time trying to suppress them, and undoing years of such effort requires time. But remember the well-known saying: "What you resist persists!" Unless you deal with the memories, so that your brain can store them away as completed "files" ("This was nasty, it happened and now it's over"), they often continue to affect you and your outlook on life. They need to be confronted, which requires a lot of bravery on your part.

This exercise makes dealing with painful recollections easier: watching the experience on an imaginary television screen. So try the following:

1 Ground yourself by feeling deeply connected to the floor. Continue to breathe calmly.

2 Close your eyes and watch your own DVD of a painful memory. Sit down and observe the drama.

3 Feel the fear, the hurt, and the loneliness, but also understand that you are here to prove you survived it.

4 Watch your "movie" several times in your mind, then add compassion and awareness to your story.

5 Write the story down in your diary.

6 See what you have learned through this experience, and mark the day that you have been able to close the movie show.

Letting go of past events is vitally important. Even so, you may find that you always have a tender spot, like a mental scar, that you have to adjust to living with. Everybody has such scars; it's part and parcel of being human.

EXTENDED MOUNTAIN MEDITATION/ VISUALIZATION
(FOR A SIMPLER VERSION, SEE PAGES 146–7)

Discovering how to deal with difficult experiences is an important skill. Now that you are integrating mindfulness, you are ready to do everything with more awareness and consequently with less harm towards yourself and others. The past is history and the future is unknown – the present is the gift!

If you feel the need to make amends, do so with gentle awareness and compassion, letting go of guilt and all the while being conscious of how "unaware" you were previously. Try the following meditation of strength and gentleness, and feel for yourself how it affects your well-being.

1 *Picture the most beautiful mountain you know or can imagine.* Notice its overall shape, the tall peak, the base rooted in the rock of the Earth's crust, the slanting sides. Note how massive the mountain is, how unmoving, and how beautiful.

2 *See whether you can bring the mountain into your own body.* Your head becomes the lofty peak, your shoulders and arms the sides of the mountain, your buttocks and legs the solid base rooted to your cushion on the floor, or to your chair.

3 *Become the breathing mountain, unwavering in your stillness, completely what you are.* Beyond words and thought, you are a centred, rooted, unmoving presence.

4 *As the light changes, as night follows day, and day night, the mountain just sits, simply being itself.* It remains still as the seasons flow into one another and as the weather changes moment by moment. Storms may come, but still the mountain sits.

5 *Imagine the mountain in springtime.* See the blue sky, with scattered clouds and the warm rays of the sun shining down. Imagine nature in springtime: the soft green leaves, multicoloured buds, birds, and the first sign of insects scattering through nature, earth, and air. The mountain remains through all this – still and abiding.

6 *Visualize a rich summer's night.* Full moon; the sound of crickets, frogs, toads, and an owl; the rich fragrance of roses and other blooms lies heavily in the air; a gentle breeze touches the bushes, the leaves in the trees, and the grass. The mountain remains through all this – still and abiding.

7 *Create a rainy autumn day in your mind.* Heavy clouds, the heavens opening, multicoloured leaves scattered around. Imagine the soundscape; hear the strong gusts of wind. The mountain remains – still and abiding.

8 *Visualize the mountain in winter.* Snowflakes are slowly covering the empty trees and the slopes of the mountain: still, calmness, white serenity.

9 *See the change in all the seasons.* Amongst all this change, the mountain abides, stillness within.

You may wish to translate the story of the mountain into your own life. And of course you may have your own ideas, and you should feel free to add or reject images and aspects of this meditation: your own mountain might have a rounded, soft peak, for example; you might want to visualize it in the morning, at lunchtime, and at night. Be creative and feel free.

The message is this: whatever life presents – beauty and challenges – deep within people can remain calm and grounded. Of course, doing so requires practice and continuity.

HOME PRACTICE FOR SESSION 5

- Practise sitting meditation, including Awareness of Sound, Body Sensation, and Breath Meditation (pages 136–7) and Difficult Thoughts Meditation (pages 138–41). If you wish, record your practice routine and your reactions to it on the record form pages 280–1.

- Practise Using the Three-Minute Breathing Space to Cope with Difficulties (see pages 270–1) whenever you notice yourself starting to feel stressed. And explore the options of responding with greater mindfulness, and in a more friendly way, to yourself and the situation.

- Bring awareness to moments of reacting, and try to respond with greater acceptance and creativity. Do this during your meditation practice too. Use the breath to bring you to this moment and to anchor you.

- Practise everyday mindfulness.

HOME-PRACTICE RECORD FORM

You can record your comments on this form each time you practise and make a note of anything that comes up in your homework, so that you can compare and contrast how each day and each practice is a new experience.

DAY/DATE	PRACTICE

COMMENTS

Session 6:
thoughts are not facts

"It is the mark of an educated mind to be able to entertain a thought without accepting it."

ARISTOTLE

Automatic thoughts can have a powerful effect on the way we feel and what we do. They aren't mystical, fantastical, incomprehensible things – they occur just beneath the surface of awareness and often lead to rumination, daydreaming, list-making, and so on. We have already looked at thoughts in Session 4, where you were introduced to NATs (see pages 258–60): negative automatic thoughts that can swiftly change your well-being and can drive you into worry, sadness, and low mood. Even if you're not aware of it, such thoughts and feelings are altered by passing time and by changes that occur during this time. Their intensity and

power over you may already have diminished; and you may have gained new insights.

By becoming aware, over and over again, of the thoughts and images passing through your mind, and by letting go of them as you return your attention to the breath and the moment, it is possible to get some distance and perspective on them. Eventually you come to understand that all thoughts are mental events, and that thoughts are neither facts, nor are we our thoughts.

Here are some ways to handle challenging thoughts. When you become aware of NATs, bring to them an attitude of gentle curiosity and ask:

- Am I confusing a thought with a fact?

- Am I jumping to conclusions?

- Am I thinking in absolute, all-or-nothing terms?

Above: *Approach NATs (negative automatic thoughts) with an air of curiosity, remembering that "thoughts are not facts".*

- Am I condemning myself because of one mistake that I made?

- Am I focusing only on my weaknesses and never on my strengths?

- Am I blaming myself for something that was not my fault?

- Am I setting standards for myself that are too high, so that I am likely to fail?

- Am I predicting the future based on past failures?

- Am I expecting to have a perfect outcome?

- Am I overestimating disaster?

A few more thoughts on thoughts

You can truly free yourself up if you learn to understand that your thoughts *are* just thoughts. Let's assume you have prepared a "to-do list" of actions that you absolutely must finish today. Then consider the story of John, who had already had his first heart attack, and of course was trying to avoid another one. At midnight one day he suddenly came to his senses: he was washing his car, and he remembered having done

---

Recognizing your thoughts as thoughts can set you free.

---

this many times. How bad could it get? What else did he have to suffer before he realized that he needed to let some things simply be (particularly at midnight!)?

Have you ever done anything similar to this? Do you, too, feel that, once you have compiled a list, it *must* be completed? It may be that, with the help of mindful awareness, you can learn to prioritize and let go. In fact, recognizing your thoughts *as* thoughts can set you free.

Right: *With the help of mindful awareness you can gradually learn to let go of your "to do" list.*

When we meditate we enter a state of "non-doing": focusing on the breath, on sound, on scanning the body or really tasting an apple. In this way you may be able to learn to simply be – just as you did when you were a small child – and may even be able to let go of guilt and shame.

Last but not least

Should you experience destructive thoughts and emotions and feel overpowered by them, you can reduce their impact by watching them as if you were standing behind a waterfall. This will offer you the chance to look at them from a safe vantage point, because the strong flow of water acts like barrier. You will experience a sense of ease simply by naming the destructive emotions: for example, "There is sadness, fear, guilt, anxiety, stress, anger, uncertainty", and so on. You can then let your thoughts be. They are simply present in your awareness and cannot drag you down. This technique was first introduced to Western meditation by Joseph Goldstein, one of the best-known Buddhist meditation teachers in the US, and is extremely helpful.

Below: *Reduce the negative impact of destructive thoughts and emotions by viewing them from a save vantage point, perhaps as if from behind a waterfall.*

HOME PRACTICE FOR SESSION 6

- Practise for 45 minutes each day over the next six days, working with different combinations of the exercises you have learned so far. You could experiment with different exercises on different days; at different times of the day; splitting the practice into two shorter sessions; and bringing different exercises into the same session.

- Practise the Three-Minute Breathing Space (see page 249) three times a day. Either practise it when you think of it, or connect it to three regular activities that you do, or to places you visit every day (for example, on waking up and/ or going to bed; before a programme that you regularly watch; before eating; after washing your hands; on first sitting down in your car or on the bus, or at your desk).

- Practise Using the Three-Minute Breathing Space to Cope with Difficulties (see pages 270–1) whenever you notice yourself starting to feel stressed. And explore the options of responding with greater mindfulness, and in a more friendly way, to yourself and the situation.

- Notice how you are relating to your thoughts day-to-day.

HOME-PRACTICE RECORD FORM

You can record your comments on this form each time you practise and make a note of anything that comes up in your homework, so that you can compare and contrast how each day and each practice is a new experience.

DAY/DATE	PRACTICE

COMMENTS

Session 7: how can I best take care of myself?

"Learn to share your love with others, but keep part of this love for yourself."

PAULO COELHO

The key aim of this session is to support your reconnection to activities and interests in your life that you may have given up or put on hold in order to create more space for work and responsibilities.

First of all, use a page in your diary and write down the events of an average workday, from the moment you wake up to the moment you switch off your light to go to sleep, as follows:

- Waking up and stretching

- Getting up and looking out of the window

- Having a shower

- Brushing my teeth

And so on . . .

Once you have finished this, review all your actions and note which ones nourish you, which are neutral, and which deplete you. You could use symbols such as ☺ , ☹, and 0 to code them, if you like.

I am sure you know just how easily you can get caught up in the bustle of daily duties, leaving no time for yourself. And when you do get a moment to relax, the temptation is probably to spend it in non-productive or even unhealthy ways, such as slumping for long periods in front of your computer or TV. As a result you need to ensure that you create time that is deliberately reserved for recharging your well-being. If you put things off until free time miraculously appears, you're going to have to wait for eternity.

What we actually *do* with our time – from moment to moment, from hour to hour, from one year to the next – can be a very powerful influence, affecting our general health and our ability to respond skilfully to the challenges in our lives. By being actually present in more of our moments, and making mindful decisions about what we really need at that time, we can improve our equilibrium and reduce our stress levels. As Jon Kabat-Zinn says, we need to weave our survival parachute, day in and day out, so that it is ready when the emergency arises. The more we arrange regular mindfulness practice, and apply awareness to everyday activities, the less we will drop our practice when the going gets rough. We need to reach a certain level of regular training – like that of daily tooth-brushing – so that we won't drop out when difficulties occur.

Enjoy exercising

Exercise is one of the best ways to look after both your physical and your mental well-being. It doesn't need to involve expensive gym membership; instead try the following:

• Aim for four brisk 15-minute walks each week.

• Include any of the following:
  Yoga
  Qigong
  T'ai chi
  Swimming
  Dancing
  Pilates
  Cycling
  Physical house-work, such as hoovering, dusting, gardening

And so on . . .

Above: *Regular exercise improves not only your physical well-being, but also your mental well-being.*

The Three-Minute Breathing Space (see page 249) offers a reminder to use mindfulness to cope with unpleasant or challenging times as they arise. But the main message is to use your awareness to help you make the best choices for coping with each difficult moment. What you opt for is unique to you.

Research proves that mindfulness helps people to recover from burnout and illnesses of both body and mind. The UK's National Institute for Clinical Health and Excellence (NICE) and the Mental Health Foundation encourage people to develop mindfulness skills, so that they can prevent illness or help themselves heal more quickly.

Enjoy life

Below is a list of activities that will provide you with joy, a sense of achievement, and of mindfulness.

It is also very important to eat a balanced diet to assist your sense of wellness: make sure you consume wholemeal carbohydrates, seven (ideally) or more portions of fresh fruit and vegetables a day, protein, and plenty of water to drink.

● **Pleasurable activities**
Have a nice hot bath or shower; take a power-nap; open the

window and breathe some fresh air; go out to your favourite restaurant or café; treat yourself to a massage, a facial, or reflexology treatment.

Start your day ten minutes early and prepare "breakfast for a king/queen"; go for a walk with a friend or visit/phone one; engage in your favourite hobby; engage in exercise (see page 291); spend time with someone you like; cook a special meal; watch something funny or uplifting on your television or computer; read something that gives you pleasure; listen to music that makes you feel good; enjoy the natural beauty around you. Sing; dance!

● **Satisfying activities**

Tidy up; spring-clean your home; send people you love a handwritten card or letter; get something done that you have been putting off for far too long.

● **Mindful activities**

Bring awareness to any given moment as often as you think of it: "Now I am washing my hands . . . now I am switching off the tap . . . now I am drying my hands – they smell lovely and feel soft." Bring attention to your breathing when you are engaged in activities, versus just "being"; bring awareness to your feet feeling connected with the ground that you are standing and moving on.

Whenever you engage in an activity, let it unfold naturally, without having any fixed expectations, for the "Tao" (life's energy) will take care of it. Be full of childlike curiosity: life is full of surprises. Surprise yourself by trying many new things, rather than getting stuck in a rut.

Mindfulness will be your best friend in times of trouble. When you are under pressure you probably tend to revert to old habits of behaving and thinking.

The more "tuned in" you are to yourself and the world about you, the wiser your decisions and actions will be. Ask yourself kindly and with compassion: "What wise action is most likely to help me through this difficulty?"

The connection between actions and moods

Remember that everything is transient and passes at last. Feeling upset because your friend doesn't arrive on time, for example, is understandable. Shouting at him when he does manage to arrive could prove to be the opposite of helpful. Ask yourself first what might have gone wrong before you judge him. What if his mobile was out of charge, or his transport broke down or did not show up? If you have judged him too swiftly, the rest of your meeting will surely not be pleasant. So let mindful action and speech be your guides. When he turns up, concentrate on your breathing and ground yourself. Then listen with awareness and compassion to the story that he shares with you. Then you will know whether his action makes sense or whether you need to tell him how disappointed you were. He is more likely to listen to you if you have given him a chance to explain and respond empathically to you.

Even if your mood has been affected by a long, uncertain wait, as best as you can, apply non-judgemental, compassionate awareness. And even if you don't manage to do so this time, you can always practise it next time. This experience is part of the human condition. Maybe, at the next opportunity, you can apply a more mindful response.

You will need time to develop this new way of responding, but slowly you will begin to notice a softening towards your own flaws and those of others. With this gentleness, you may learn to embrace life's experiences – even those that you may not have handled well in the past.

HOME PRACTICE FOR SESSION 7

- Choose a couple of exercises from among all the different mindfulness meditations that you have been introduced to throughout the course. Practise them daily if at all possible, plus one extra exercise every week. And feel free to continue noting down anything of interest in your diary.

- Practise the Three-Minute Breathing Space (see page 249) regularly, and as an intervention when you need it.

- Watch out for warning signs that you are feeling stressed, anxious, angry, or depressed when things are difficult. Note down an action plan that you can use once you have noticed the early warning signs. For example, you might listen to a mindfulness-meditation recording; remind yourself of what you're learning in this book; read a poem or a story that might "reconnect" you with your "wiser" mind.

HOME-PRACTICE RECORD FORM

You can record your comments on this form each time you practise and make a note of anything that comes up in your homework, so that you can compare and contrast how each day and each practice is a new experience.

DAY/DATE	PRACTICE

COMMENTS

Session 8: living mindfully for the rest of your days

"There are two ways to wash dishes: One is to wash them in order to make them clean; the other is to wash them in order to wash them."

ANTHONY DE MELLO

Mindfulness can become second nature to you, with regular practise and by maintaining a mindset of openness, childlike curiosity, non-judgement, and patience. With the right attitude you will learn to change into a kinder person.

The advantages of awareness, acceptance, and mindfully *responding* to situations – rather than immediately running off knee-jerk, pre-programmed "automatic" reactions – have been a recurring theme throughout this eight-session course. The acceptance of what *is* will help you to respond skilfully to challenges, rather than react aggressively or fearfully.

Above: *When you have a mindful conversation you really listen and only talk when a natural pause occurs.*

MINDFUL-VIEWING PRACTICE

Here is a short exercise that you will be able to carry out almost anywhere – even a bare white wall will do as your point of focus.

1 Find a window, a plant, or an object at home or in your office; stop in front of a shop window, a tree, a bush, or any other appealing item. Now resolve in your mind that for the next few minutes you are only going to gaze at this one chosen viewpoint. Decide not to let your eyes wander.

2 Notice how many details you can find in this one point of focus. It is amazing how sometimes things change within your viewpoint (for example, when you look out of a window, nature might bring different visitors into that frame). Even if you choose an empty white wall, you may notice little cracks, dots, and shadows. Bring patience and curiosity to this practice. For once, your eyes will not be forced to deal with overload.

3 Ground yourself at the beginning and end of the exercise. To do so, perhaps you can feel into your body and see whether the simple act of "watching something" can change the experience of the moment and the energy flow in your body.

DAILY MINDFULNESS

1 When you first wake up in the morning, before you get out of bed, bring your attention to your breathing. Observe five mindful breaths.

2 Be aware of how your body and mind feel when you move from lying down to sitting, to standing and to walking. Notice how it feels each time you make a transition from one posture to the next.

3 Whenever you hear a phone ring, a bird sing, a train pass by, laughter, a car horn, the wind, the sound of a door closing, use that sound like the bell of mindfulness. Really listen, feeling present and awake.

4 Throughout the day take a few moments to bring your attention to your breathing. At these times, observe five mindful breaths.

5 Whenever you eat or drink something, take a minute and breathe. Look at your food and realize that it was connected to something that nourished its growth. Can you see in your food the sunlight, the rain, the earth, the farmer, the lorry-driver – all the elements and people that helped to produce it? Pay attention as you eat, consciously consuming this food for your physical health. Bring awareness to seeing your food, smelling your food, tasting your food, chewing your food, and swallowing your food.

6 Pay attention your body while you are walking or standing. Take a moment to notice your posture. Pay attention to the contact of the ground under your feet. Feel the air on your face, arms, and legs as you walk. Ask yourself, are you rushing?

7 Bring awareness to listening and talking. When listening, can you listen without agreeing or disagreeing, liking or disliking, or planning what you will say when it is your turn? When talking, can you just say what you need to say, without overstating or understating? Can you notice how your mind and body feel?

8 Whenever you are waiting in a queue, use the time to notice your standing and breathing. Feel the contact of your feet on the floor and notice the way your body feels. Bring attention to the rising and falling of your abdomen. Ask yourself, are you feeling impatient?

9 Be aware of any tightness in your body throughout the day. Breathe into it and, as you exhale, let go of excess tension. Is there tension stored in your neck, shoulders, stomach, jaw, or lower back? If possible, stretch or do yoga/mindful walking once a day.

10 Focus attention on your daily activities – such as brushing your teeth, brushing your hair, washing up, putting on your shoes, doing your job. Bring mindfulness to each activity.

11 Before you go to sleep at night, take a few minutes and bring your attention to your breathing. Observe five mindful breaths. Write down in your diary what you enjoyed today, what you were grateful for and satisfied with.

(ADAPTED FROM: MADDY KLYNE, INSTRUCTOR, UNIVERSITY OF MASSACHUSETTS MEDICAL CENTER, USA)

Last, but not least

Write down and consider your answers to the following questions:

- What sacrifices did you have to make – if any – to do this course?

- What do you expect to be the biggest obstacles in your ongoing mindfulness practice?

- What insights have you gained to help yourself get unstuck, if you stop practising?

MINDFULNESS IN ALL WALKS OF LIFE

Living mindfully is not a quick panacea or a swift takeaway that you can use to cure a current issue. On the contrary, rather than being a quick fix, mindful living invites you to be aware, kind, compassionate, and all-inclusive for the rest of your life. If more and more individuals were to create a mindful society, then we would not need to wait for a miracle to change all suffering on Earth. Our planet would alter for the better, and suffering would gradually reduce. So if you want to change the world, all you need do is change yourself, allowing this transition to unfold gradually, gently and, most of all, peacefully.

Right: *Mindful living is the first step to creating a better society and encouraging positive change in the world.*

Living mindfully

It all starts with the notion that every single one of us experiences suffering, fear, joy, hunger, and so on, so we are all in this together.

This is why you are invited to apply all the insights and skills you have picked up by reading this book to every step you take throughout the day. You will invariably start with mindfulness at home.

Waking and getting up mindfully

When you wake up, breathe in kindness and joy and, on breathing out, let go of any worries for the day. Just stay with your breathing and the simple joy of having another day in which to be alive. The way you enter your morning sets you up with the right attitude for the rest of the day. So start the day by noticing how your body and mind are feeling. Can you feel any

particular emotions in your body and, if so, can you name them? Gently ask yourself what is occupying your mind most intensely. If you tend to do your longer meditations in the afternoon or evening, still focus for a few minutes on simply noticing your breath as soon as you wake up.

When you are in the shower, truly feel the temperature of the water on your skin, and notice the smell of your shower gel or shampoo. Mindfully dry your body and hair, kindly and patiently. Could you possibly smile, right down into your body?

When you're making breakfast for yourself and/or others, think about the purpose of taking care of yourself and others, now and throughout the

day. When preparing and eating your breakfast (and any meal, for that matter), enjoy it with all your senses: feel the texture, enjoy the smell, the taste, and how a number of different items can be combined to make a tasty concoction. As best you can, eat each mouthful feeling utterly alert, and see how many of the different ingredients are noticeable.

Whatever household chores may be waiting for you – prior to going to work or constituting your work – try as best you can to engage mindfully with every action and you may find some enjoyable aspect to it. Then add a little gratitude: when washing up, for example, enjoy the warm water and the lovely smell of the liquid soap, without feeling resentment at having to do it. Thich Nhat Hanh describes in *The Miracle of Mindfulness* the challenges of washing up with cold water. Here is a brief summary taken from that book: "When I was still a novice, washing the hundred dishes was hardly a pleasant task . . . There was no soap. We had ashes and rice husks . . . during winter the water was freezing . . . It is easier to enjoy washing the dishes now: liquid soap, scrub pads and running hot water."

> Whatever household chores may be waiting for you, try as best you can to engage mindfully with every action and you may find some enjoyable aspect to it.

If there are pets or family members in the house, before you leave make sure you say an intentional goodbye – if possible, making eye contact and connecting with them in your heart.

Left: *When you wake up, notice how your body and mind are feeling. The way you start your day can influence how the rest of it evolves.*

ORDER IN EVERYTHING

If you ever doubt that you are special and part of the creative universe, then just read the following poem by the writer and meditator Max Eames:

Meant to Be

As the light danced on the water,
I realized in a flash
That there was order in
   everything;
Not a thing was out of place.
The pizza box, with its wet
   splodge of grease;
The casually discarded beach
   towel;
The blob of ice cream, frozen
   in suspended animation
As it dribbled toward the waves;
Somehow wishing, like me, to
   be idly swept away.
A wave of healing washed
   over me,
And it made me laugh, smile,
   and stifle a tear
All at the same time.
Nothing, not a bit of it, was
   out of place;
Not even me. I was exactly
   where I was meant to be,
And to sustain my denial seemed
A profoundly foolish act;
One of squandering
What I had been bestowed.

MAX EAMES

CASE STUDY
KITTY, 40

To begin with, having read many of the published benefits of mindfulness, I was determined to practise formal sitting for the length of time recommended week by week of the eight-week course. I knew I needed mindfulness to help me manage my anxiety and depression, and I knew I had to practise regularly for it to "work". Left alone, my mind would wander off along habitual and destructive paths that were feeding my depression.

Many teachers explain that training the mind is like training a puppy, to stop it getting into trouble. For me, it was more like training a wild animal. My teacher invited me to be aware of thoughts, and of the spaces between them. "There are spaces between thoughts? What spaces?" I asked. So I needed the discipline of sitting and listening to guidance from a teacher, to enable me to begin the repetitive work of noticing my mind wandering off and to bring it back.

Alongside the formal mindfulness practices, I was also learning to carry out daily activities with awareness of their sensory aspects. I needed triggers and reminders, or my mind would set off down a well-worn track – often either harmful or useless – depleting my energy, lowering my mood, and preventing me from appreciating the simple pleasures of life.

With this daily practice came increased self-awareness and an observation of cause and effect: "If I do this, this happens; and if I do that, that happens." For example, before mindfulness, I would drink copious amounts of tea and coffee and suffer anxiety symptoms; on autopilot, the connection between caffeine and anxiety was not apparent to me. Mindfulness enabled me to gain more control of my life and make wiser decisions as to how I choose to spend my time and what I drink.

Now, as my experience of mindfulness increases, I enjoy those times when I can meet other practitioners for longer periods of practice, to maintain the depth of my experience. In between, I practise formally and informally, with formal practice depending on my diary. I will often head to bed earlier than normal, to practise in the evening, if I have had a full day at work. It always amazes me what can come up from the depths of my mind in a meditation sitting – often useful insights that I know I would not have thought of had I not been meditating.

I now have a tool to help me "steer a steady course" through life's difficulties, and to "be with" occasional low moods and feelings of anxiety without fear of relapse. I am more resilient and self-reliant, rather than feeling the need to search for other people who will make me well. When I go without practising for any length of time I miss the feelings of joy, peace, and connectedness that mindfulness reveals. Mindfulness is life-changing, as many other people have found. I recommend anybody to try it and discover this for themselves.

Getting ready for daily challenges

When you set out to travel to work, red traffic lights can be used as a reminder to be mindful on the road and not move completely into autopilot. Are you still grounded and aware of your surroundings? If not, take a few mindful breaths. If you are driving a car, really feel your feet on the pedals and your hands on the steering wheel.

Whatever form of transport you take, you can try *not* to listen to music at times, but instead to focus your awareness on the sounds that are coming and going. If you work from home, try this before turning on your computer. Exposing yourself to choices and acting on them feels good and primes your mind for the rest of the day.

As best you can, treat all experiences during your day in a mindful way, using the Three-Minute Breathing Space (see page 249) whenever you feel things are getting too much for you.

Below: *As you drive to work in the morning, be mindful of the feeling of your hands on the steering wheel.*

ENJOYING SILENCE

Listening to nature is a practice that is particularly suitable for everyday life. Treasures, big and small, show up throughout the day and can become reminders for this practice, which can be done anywhere. Read the following poem:

Stormy Rain

Drop
Drop, drop
Another drop
Abundant more dripping drops
Draining, flooding, pouring,
    rumbling
Soaking deep green earthen
    pastures
Welling up, muddy, gooey,
    doughy, sinking paths
Sliding, weeping, gushing,
    blowing over, ripping off
    nature's heaps
Dripping drops
Drop drops
Drop.

This poem wrote itself in my mind shortly after a wild rainstorm in the Alps. I was guiding a silent retreat, and on such retreats you follow a certain formula every day. You sit in silence and then you walk in silence. Any activity is carried out in silence too. You eat in silence and neither read nor write. All electronic devices have to be switched off, as they are when taking off or landing in an aeroplane.

This may sound deeply unadventurous. However, it is amazing what can happen: first of all, on the internal canvas of your mind; and then externally, where nature can mirror the internal struggles of the mind. Silence offers us a wonderful opportunity to stop having lots of new inputs and instead deal with some aspects of "undigested" past experiences; or alternatively with micro-experiences that we are only really able to notice if we are still.

Mostly silence has a deep-cleansing effect on mind and body. And on this particular day nature had a deep-cleanse too, and it was poignant to watch and feel this wild, wet occurrence. It was like stepping into union with all that is.

If you read the poem again you will notice how it flows from the micro-action of a drop – the start of a rain shower – and (like the middle part of a symphony) builds to a torrent of rain and the response by the Earth, then peters out and finally stops. Symbolically it may help you to see that many a problem starts, peaks, and then ebbs away. Whatever it is that is causing upheaval will also pass.

Enjoying life

Here are other examples of everyday occurrences that people who practise mindfulness regularly have reported.

- A magic morning: before it gets really light you might be able to hear birdsong, which is the most beautiful alternative to an alarm clock. When you turn on the tap to fill the kettle, be mindful: notice the soft, cool water as it flows into the vessel or as individual droplets touch your skin; maybe you will feel a sense of gratitude arise. Just listen, rise slowly, and enjoy your first cup of coffee as you watch how the sun's pure light floods the horizon.

- Eating more slowly and focusing on eating alone. Avoiding reading the newspaper or watching TV while having dinner. Maybe even experimenting with foods that you might not have touched before.

- Drinking tea or coffee with true focus and pleasure. You will find it easier not to drink too much (see Kitty's story on pages 309–10), and yet those few cups will be deeply enjoyable. Perhaps buy a new teapot and cup so that you can celebrate a little tea ceremony. Let it become a ritual you look forward to immensely. Purchase different tea flavours and almost feel as if you were participating in a wine-tasting. It is fun and playful and can make you feel more peaceful at the end.

Other areas of life that call out for mindfulness

- Giving up "running after" various forms of transport. Sooner or later there will be another train, bus, or tube train. Move with more awareness and you will notice more "moments" while you are on your excursions. Every opportunity can bring new surprises. Standing in a queue becomes cumbersome no longer. Every experience is truly unique and worth having.

- Being more attentive when others talk to you. Also being more mindful of how you want to reply, and choosing your words with compassion. Avoid words of judgement and anger, finger-pointing, and being bitter.

- Dealing with anger: if you are annoyed because of somebody's actions, attempt to ground yourself and breathe in and out for a few moments. Close your eyes and become aware that sooner or later this situation will have lost its drama. Find a way to be assertive and to share your hurt. By not attacking there is a chance that the person who offended you might find it in their heart to apologize.

- Self-compassion: become aware that it is part of the human condition to make mistakes. Do not use this as an excuse, but as an insight. From here you may find the right way of looking towards more compassionate action, and a determination not to do wrong again – in so far as this is possible. Gently place one hand on your heart and the other on one of your cheeks; then give yourself a hug (thereby increasing production of the "compassion hormone" oxytocin) and feel the "tender gravity of kindness".

- Turning your bathroom into your own spa retreat. You might want to invest in new potions and lotions, or even make them yourself. Candles and gentle music can really turn a bath into an experience of pure relaxation. Watch out for the mind wanting to make lists, and refuse to listen to these "automatic thoughts". Try telling yourself: This can wait until later.

- Treating yourself to reflexology, a facial, Pilates, a massage, or yoga classes – because you're worth it!

Have you thought of anything else you could add to this list? Step by step, and by being patient and persistent, you may reach a level of equanimity and inner peace.

Don't be surprised when people start noticing that something has changed. More smiles may be exchanged with others. You may even buy your colleagues or neighbours some little gifts (no pressure – just a thought).

Below: *Caring for your body is a form of mindfulness.*

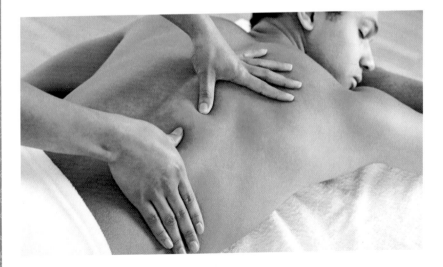

HEAVENLY TEA

Buddha Maitreya is a man who not only believes that he has reached enlightenment, but has also been awarded prizes for his Japanese garden in Nottinghamshire – the Pure Land Japanese Garden – which is the most delightful of its kind in the UK. After walking through the garden and listening to how the wise man sees the world and human existence, you may be invited to afternoon tea. He serves heavenly scones and heavenly tea.

He makes these lovely little cakes out of a (secret) mixture of flours, and his tea from a number of green teas to which he adds flowers, herbs, and spices. The tea is light and yet it delivers something heavenly indeed – each sip you take seems to hit different tastebuds: sometimes it's sharp, then sweet, flowery, and scented. Do try and experience it.

MINDFULNESS IN ALL WALKS OF LIFE

Drinking tea

The twentieth-century Viennese writer Peter Altenberg tells the following story about the joy and deep satisfaction of drinking tea.

Six o'clock in the evening is approaching. I can sense it drawing near. Not quite as intensely as children feel Christmas Eve, but creeping up all the same. At six o'clock on the dot I drink tea, a celebratory enjoyment devoid of disappointment in this ailing existence. Something that makes you realize that you have the power of calming happiness in your hands. Even the action of pouring fresh water into my beautiful, wide half-litre nickel kettle gives me pleasure. I wait patiently for it to boil, listening out for the whistling sound, the singing of the water.

I have a huge, deep, round mug made of red-brick-coloured Wedgwood. The tea from Café Central smells like meadows in the countryside.

The tea has a golden-yellow hue, like fresh hay. It never gets too brown, but remains light and delicate. I drink it mindfully and very slowly. The tea has a stimulating effect on my nervous system. Everything in life seems to be more bearable and lighter thereafter.

Drinking my tea at six o'clock never seems to lose its power over me. Every day I long for it as intensely as the day before, and when I drink it I lovingly embrace it into my being.

(TRANSLATED AND ADAPTED BY PATRIZIA COLLARD FROM *SONNENUNTERGANG IM PRATER* BY PETER ALTENBERG)

Tea for one

George Orwell was a fervent tea drinker, adamant that milk should be added only after the tea was poured. Here are a few other tea-drinking "essentials" that he prescribed, from an article published in the *Evening Standard*, 12 January 1946:

- Use Indian or Ceylonese tea.

- Make tea in a teapot.

- Warm the pot beforehand.

- The tea should be strong and put straight into the pot.

- Give the pot a good shake.

- Use a cylindrical cup.

- Pour tea into the cup first and drink without sugar.

When you make your next cup of tea, you may want to carry out this whole "ritual" mindfully.

Above: *The famous writer George Orwell loved tea and wrote a whole article on how to brew it just right.*

MINDFULNESS IN ALL WALKS OF LIFE

TAKE A MINDFUL AFTERNOON BREAK

How about creating an Austrian *Konditorei* (cake shop) at home, maybe once a month? A wonderful *café mélange* (see opposite) is made out of fresh ground coffee and hot milk. It is a little stronger than a *café latte* and is always served with a glass of water to counterbalance the dehydrating effects of the coffee. Accompany it with real, homemade Viennese *Apfelstrudel* (see recipe opposite).

Café mélange

Ideally you should use a silver Italian coffee pot, into which you put ground coffee with ground figs, heating it up until the water slowly rises. The milk has to be beaten until it is hot and frothy. Pour the coffee into a large, flat cup and slowly spoon in the milk, making sure none of the froth is lost. Finally, add a sprinkle of dark chocolate powder on top.

Apfelstrudel

1. Quarter and core 750g (1½lb) dessert apples and carefully cut them into thin slices. Put the apples in a bowl and add 100g (3½oz) raisins, 75g (3oz) fresh white breadcrumbs, 50g (2oz) soft light brown sugar, the grated rind of 1 lemon, 50g (2oz) toasted pine nuts and 1 teaspoon ground cinnamon. Stir the mixture well.

2. Melt 65g (2½oz) unsalted butter in a small saucepan. Lay 2 sheets of chilled filo pastry from a 200 g (7 oz) packet on a lightly floured work surface, next to each other and overlapping by about 2.5 cm (1 inch) to form a larger sheet of pastry. Brush the pastry with melted butter, then top with the remaining pastry, brushing each layer with a little butter.

3. Spread the apple mixture over the pastry, leaving a 5 cm (2 inch) border. Fold the long sides over the filling. Brush with butter and roll up from a short side to form a log-shape.

4. Transfer the strudel very mindfully to a greased baking sheet, brush it with the remaining melted butter and bake in a preheated oven, 200°C (400°F), Gas Mark 6, for 30–35 minutes until lightly golden. To decorate, combine 2 tablespoons sifted icing sugar with a little extra cinnamon and dust the strudel. Serve hot with whipped cream.

Taking note

At this point I would like you to note down in your diary what changes you have observed in your daily life, behaviour, thinking patterns, use of language, and so on. Also make a plan based on whether any of the ideas given above sound soothing or adventurous. The last step, of course, is putting them into practice.

Before the day is done

Sleep is more important than you might think. Without enough sleep you may be more vulnerable to ill health, such as diabetes, heart disease, depression, and even unwanted weight gain. Furthermore, you will be less able to remember new skills or data and more likely to feel sleepy and irritable.

Do you frequently stay up too late and take drinks containing caffeine to keep you alert? And could it be that you use a gin and tonic to wind down when you come home? If you endeavour to improve your sleep, there are two important points to remember: first, instead of the quick-fix G&T, you would benefit more from practising meditation when you get back from work. This will help you let go

---

Without enough sleep you may be more vulnerable to ill health, such as diabetes, heart disease, depression, and even unwanted weight gain

---

of whatever is lurking in the office for you; it will surely still be there tomorrow, so allow this thought to pass. For the moment you need not concern yourself with anything but the *now*. Second, apply consistency, getting a really good rest every night and not trying to catch up at the weekend, for example. Really enjoy feeling rested and alert when you get enough sleep. Notice what it feels like when you are full of beans and truly refreshed.

Mindful parenthood and family life

This is a huge subject and could only be covered in all its aspects and applications if I had the space of an extra book in which to write.

So I have chosen a few stories and insights to share with you, to give you something to work on for yourself.

Mindful birthing

This real example of a birthing plan shows how to mindfully approach a potentially difficult and life-changing event. The mum-to-be in question used mindfulness and compassion skills to make the event memorable and joyful. If you manage to find the meaning in pain, it usually reduces its intensity and significance.

Above: *A newborn baby is totally mindful and perceives everything as an adventure.*

COMPASSIONATE BIRTHING PLAN

- I want to remember my baby's last scan picture. I could see its hair and it was sucking its thumb. The little one will need strength and perseverance when it is travelling from the womb through the birthing channel into the world.

- I will endeavour to tell my baby regularly how much I love it.

It already recognizes my voice and this will calm it down.

- When labour starts, it may seem as if it will take an eternity, but in reality it will be very much shorter than the nine months of pregnancy. I will soon be able to hold my little one and cuddle and kiss it.

- Each contraction is one step towards the arrival of my baby.

- I am so lucky to have been able to choose a wonderfully calm and light delivery room in which to give birth. I have collected calm music and nature sounds to play while I am in labour. I have frozen mango juice, cranberry juice, and apple and elderflower juice. These little cubes of juice will keep me going when I am focusing on delivering my baby.

I actually look forward to it more and more.

- I feel so grateful to have good support on this special day. There is pain relief available, should I feel that I need it.

- I sometimes remember how much harder it must have been for women in the past – or even now, in developing countries. They may have to travel for days to get to a hospital. More gratitude is arising, plus compassion for those who have less assistance.

- I am trying to let go of fear and invite hope and joy into my heart. My mantra will be "I can, and all will be well."

- When my baby is born, I will take it home to a beautifully decorated, warm, cosy room.

- I will slowly regain my fitness after the birth, and my body will feel lighter and more like its former self again.

- I wonder what my little one will look and be like. It is such a privilege and mystery to become a mother.

- My baby will be a newborn for a very short time, so I will do my best to enjoy every stage of its development.

- I trust that my body has a deep knowing of how to deliver my baby. I will visualize every stage of my labour and the actual moment my baby pops out, and I will hold it in my arms and kiss, stroke, and breastfeed it.

- May I be well, may I be happy, safe, and healthy, and may all things go well for me.

- May my baby be well, may my baby be happy, safe, and healthy, and may all things go well for my baby.

And for the mum who has delivered this beautiful new life into the world: treat yourself with kindness, and pamper your body! When you are offered a shower, add some beautiful rose, patchouli, or papaya shower gel. Massage it gently into your skin all over – feel the warm water, inhale the scent of the gel, appreciate the sound of the soothing flow, as if you were standing under a waterfall. Enjoy!

FINDING TIME
THE STORY OF ONE YOUNG MOTHER

The following short tale is based on a story written by K Masters and describes what one young mother did to try to carve out some more time for herself.

The young mother listened with wonder to her friends as they shared stories from their meditation or yoga classes. As she had to bring up three children all by herself, there seemed to be no way for her to take part in such classes. There was never enough money or time available. She did, however, offer one of the visiting teachers from India a guest room in her house. He soon understood her predicament, for even at home – where he would have been happy to guide her in meditation – there was always a little one who needed her help. She felt a little low, as even this opportunity was "taken from her".

One day he enquired which daily duty she spent most of her time doing. It turned out to be washing the dishes. So the next time (and often thereafter) he was right next to her while she was washing up. He invited her to be really present in this moment, where her life was actually happening. "Feel the water, how hot it is, and how your hands hold onto each dish and the cloth cleans them. Bring awareness to your posture, and even to your breathing and how it changes when you are physically active." Thus washing up became her mindfulness practice for many years, until her kids were old enough for her to attend meetings and retreats.

Having read this story, you can see that life can be lived mindfully moment by moment, and that the formal practices are only the preparation for leading a mindful, peaceful, and compassionate existence, day by day.

Mindful parenting practice

You are woken at 4am the night before a long day of work awaits you. Notice your thoughts, such as "I could do without this . . . I am so tired." Now turn your attention and kindly awareness to the child lying close to you – the small delicate form, who is sleeping peacefully, feeling safe because of your closeness. The child is asleep . . . so perhaps a dream woke you, or a distant noise. Now let go of feeling constricted – keep looking at your child. Remember this time will soon pass. Really observe your child's beautiful features, smooth skin, hair, eyes, hands . . . What else do you notice? Their unique scent, the rhythmic childlike sound of their breathing, and the softness you feel when you touch their head. What are your thoughts now? What do you notice in your emotions, and physically in your body? Drink in the warm feelings of love and appreciate this miracle. Feel kindness arise, despite your tiredness, and let it reside in the background of your awareness. Be still, now, in this exquisite moment.

Drink in the warm feelings of love and appreciate this miracle. Feel kindness arise.

This little person is actually a fully developed human being – the only difference from a grown-up is their shorter life experience. They have their very own personality, likes and dislikes, talents, strengths, and weaknesses. As the Lebanese poet and writer Kahlil Gibran said, you are the bow and they are the arrows. If you have learned to know and understand them deeply, you can shoot them in the right direction and give them a good and secure start.

MINDFULNESS IN ALL WALKS OF LIFE

THE GRANNY ON RETREAT

On a week-long Thich Nhat Hanh family retreat, a granny was deepening her mindfulness practice and shared with younger retreatants her experience as a busy mum who mainly worked, cleaned, cooked, washed, and worried, and thus was always on autopilot, thinking and planning. She realized she had missed out on so much of her children growing up. Now, being a grandmother and practising mindfulness, she was in a way catching up with what she had missed. Now she was fully present with her grandchildren and their development: stories, imaginative games, kindergarten, school – you name it. She rediscovered the world through their eyes. And what a joy it was to experience this journey (albeit briefly) with her. She was so very happy!

AND NOW: LOVE THYSELF!

Are you worth it – the whole fallible you, simply because you are? Once you can wholeheartedly answer this question with a resounding "yes", you have started to comprehend mindfulness and compassion.

Read the following poem a few times and then pin it up in a place where you can peruse it several times a day.

Just for Me

....

What if a poem were just
  for me?
What if I were audience enough
    because I am,
Because this person here is alive,
    is flesh,
Is conscious, has feelings,
    counts?
What if this one person mattered
    not just for what

She can do in the world
But because she is part of
    the world
And has a soft and tender heart?
What if that heart mattered,
If kindness to this one mattered?
What if she were not distinct
    from all others,
But instead connected to others
    in her sense of being distinct,
    of being alone,
Of being uniquely isolated,
    the one piece removed from
    the picture –
All the while vulnerable under,
    deep under, the layers of
    sedimentary defence.

Oh, let me hide
Let me be ultimately great,
Ultimately shy,
Remove me, then I don't
    have to . . .
be . . .
But I am.

Through all the antics of
　　distinctness from others,
　　or not-really-there-ness,
　　I remain
No matter what my disguise –
Genius, idiot, gloriousness,
　　scum –
Underneath, it's still just me,
　　still here,

Still warm and breathing
　　and human
With another chance simply
　　to say hi, and recognize
　　my tenderness
And be just a little bit kind
　　to this one as well,
Because she counts, too.

ANON.

Mindfulness in relationships

Practising mindfulness regularly can help you see situations from another person's perspective.

What a wonderful gift this is for loving relationships. When you date someone, or even live with them, close proximity to that other person may at times feel a little tight. Seeing a problem from their perspective can help you both live peacefully together.

Mindful tools include:

- **Thinking before you speak**. Take a pause and consider whether what you are about to say will really help both parties. Try to choose soft words and a kind facial expression, and you are more likely to be listened to. Use mindful pauses to let the information sink in. Pay attention not only to what you are saying, but also to *how* you are saying it.

- **Keeping your eyes wide open**. Let go of looking at your partner in a habitual fashion. Recall what it is that you find really special about him or her and look at them with a fresh perspective; maybe even tell them how you love their new haircut, lipstick, and so on. Or just say, "I really love your smile" or "I love the colour of your eyes".

- **Listening mindfully**. It is heart-warming when somebody really listens to you, with interest and with an open mind. So just listen to your partner, and do not prepare your reply while you are listening. Really look at your partner with open-mindedness.

• **Preparing a romantic meeting from time to time.** Long-term relationships can fall into a rut, especially if both parties work, or if there are a number of children or pets to look after. "Foreplay" starts 24 hours before being intimate with your partner. Write a note, buy some theatre or cinema tickets, cook a lovely meal, or go to a special restaurant. Tell your partner how much you are looking forward to your time together. Make an effort to look ravishing, and enjoy being playful and seductive. This is your beloved: she or he deserves to be cherished and bestowed with gifts.

Love conquers all

In the beautiful novel *If Only It Were True (Et si c'était vrai)* by Marc Levy a man finds a woman in his bathroom cupboard. Strangely, she turns out to be the spirit of a young female doctor who lies in a coma in a nearby hospital and is close to having her life-support machine switched off. He wants to help her, because he's the only living being who can see that she is still alive. So he decides to kidnap her body and persuades his best friend to help him do so. His friend, alas, cannot see or hear the woman, but still helps, simply because he trusts the man totally. Even though the friend's first reaction is one of disbelief, he responds to the man's request and helps him save the spirit of the woman, with whom he has by now fallen in love . . . I hope you get the gist! The point of the story is that true friendship is rare and will be tested at times. A real friend will have to overcome his own doubts and gift you with his trust.

Recently one of my friends was convinced that somebody in his office was planning to squash his excellent reputation, because this person was out to get his job. Nobody believed my friend – some thought

he was entering paranoia and needed mental-health assistance. But, having known my friend for 30 years, I knew he was onto something. It all sounded far-fetched, but in the end the traitor was found out, because he left his office drawers unlocked and a cleaning lady discovered lots of evidence. He had, in fact, been after several people's jobs. Now of course the cleaning lady should not

Above: *Practising mindfulness together can deepen your relationship and create a sense of belonging.*

have been looking in anybody's drawers, but she did. People are nosy, and in this particular case it saved my friend's face and ended the negative plans of the "baddy".

The best way of keeping your friendships is to overcome your doubts and trust friends to be there for you when you need them.

The Four Mantras of loving one another

I recently watched an interview between Oprah Winfrey and Thich Nhat Hanh, the Vietnamese Buddhist monk who brought mindfulness to the West. The topic of the talk was "mindful living", and it was amazing to hear how Nhat Hanh had been a friend of famous peace activists like Dr Martin

Above: *Fear can cause us to freeze emotionally. Mindfulness can slowly help us to "feel alive" again.*

Luther King, Jnr. The second half of the interview focused on relationships, and how mindfulness can help us to achieve communication and honest dialogue. Nhat Hanh described meditation as deep listening (being eager to learn and understand another point of view). If you act mindfully, you will avoid fear, anger, and hate in a relationship, which are all born of incorrect perceptions and interpretations.

When your beloved returns home from a day's work, really notice them and welcome them back. A mindful hug can soothe away the stresses of the day (I am talking here of a warm, loving hug that dissolves tension). A brief space of listening compassionately to how their day was, and vice versa, can nurture each other when the need occurs. Deep listening means finding time to be with each other, looking into their eyes; having no mobile phones around when you are preparing the meal together; sharing the meal, really eating (see page 344) together, and having a proper conversation. By sharing, you can become mutually supportive. You will be able to stand up against the world, which may often demand too much of you.

To avoid destructive emotions in loving relationships, Thich Nhat Hanh suggests using the Four Mantras.

1. **"Darling, I am here for you."** This refers to the understanding that you need to be truly and actively present for the person you love.

2. **"Darling, I know you are there."** This supports an awareness of the other person's presence and needs, which at times may differ from your own, although you still recognize them as valid.

3. **"Darling, I know you are suffering."** This is an offering of support for your beloved in times of need.

4. **"Darling, I am suffering and I truly try to practise compassion and forgiveness. Please help me do this for us."**

Our negativity bias (focusing on the negative) is so strong that we need to remember all that is – and was – good and wholesome ("taking in the good") when the going gets rough. One unpleasant situation can dominate our experience of the others, because of the somewhat "flawed" wiring of our brains. Try your best not to lose sight of what you initially fell in love with in your partner or friend. They were special enough for you to stay with them. Take in the good once more, and remember their uniqueness.

Try your best not to lose sight of what you initially fell in love with in your partner or friend.

Sometimes difficulties are more challenging and you need to make a time-slot for sitting down and being together. The key is to accept the other person's feelings, even when you do not agree with them or fully comprehend them. They might appear illogical or over-the-top, but your love commitment helps the other person to be heard and feel accepted. Together you can then try and find a way to manage the difficulty. You could ask, "What can I do to help you ease your pain?"

In a healthy, mindful relationship remember that humour (laughing, jokes), kindness, patience, and compassion need to be displayed regularly. A friend suggests, "Have a few jokes or funny memories, favourite programmes, and comedians' sayings written down, so that you can access them when your brain is too stressed to retrieve this information."

Allow laughter and smiling to lift you up

Humour is one of the best stress-releasers. You have two nervous systems: the sympathetic nervous system (see page 55), or "fight or flight" response; and the parasympathetic nervous system (see page 55), or peace state.

The first system is essential for survival, and releases stress chemicals – adrenaline, noradrenaline, and

Above: *Focus on the joy each moment can bring*

cortisol – in order to get you ready for survival. The second system is the one you ideally want to spend most of your life in: peaceful, joyful, oozing equanimity and calmness, and floating in endorphins (feel-good chemicals).

Laughter automatically switches on the latter system: you laugh, and all of a sudden you feel well. Dr

Norman Cousins describes in his book *Anatomy of an Illness* (there is also a film of his story) how he was suffering from an untreatable degenerative disease and discover that laughter gave him periods of being pain-free. Furthermore, joy became a major component of his self-created cure, which helped him back to good health. He watched humorous films, read amusing books and jokes, and doctors were baffled as to how he destroyed his illness and even repaired the damage it had already done to his body.

This is one of the best examples of well-being having a direct connection to good humour and mood. Ask yourself, and then note down in your diary what makes you giggle, and thus nourishes you.

Mindfulness in a social context

Practising mindfulness is occasionally referred to as a way of dealing better with what life – and people – throw at us.

How might mindfulness assist us in making this world a better place in which to live?

Recently the cover of *Time* magazine showed a pretty woman who, we were told, was bringing awareness to her existence in the hope of experiencing more peace in her life. I read the headline: "The Mindful Revolution: The science of finding focus in a stressed-out, multitasking culture". I do not dispute this message, but it bleaches out another, more radical one: that mindfulness practice can deliver insight.

I regularly teach mindfulness to students, employees, artists, medical personnel, and psychotherapists; to people who make laws and those who break them. I hear songs of woe referring to stress, suffering, and the fight to survive in a world that has changed so much. I learn about the many faces of anxiety and self-blame. In the West, quite differently from Eastern societies such as Nepal and Tibet, we never believe that we are "good enough", and so we need constantly to prove to ourselves that we are special. We feel we must work longer and harder, expose ourselves to more stimulation, learn how to use new gadgets on a monthly basis, if we are to keep up with others. But does any happiness arise in this frantic world? Have we reached "the point of no return" – spending sleepless nights watching the news on our "tablet" in bed? The horrors that reach us on the news (via all forms of technology) while they are happening cannot possibly leave us untouched, unless we just stuff them down or think, "Just as well I live in Europe" and then disengage from the truth, before it drives us crazy. But a certain madness is already spreading.

The outward sign of this problem is the ever-expanding rise of mental disease. According to a report published by the UK's Mental Health Foundation: "In any one year 1 in 4 British adults experience at least one mental disorder, and 1 in 6 experiences this at any given time"; and "among teenagers, rates of depression and anxiety have increased by 70% in the past 25 years" (up to 2007).

As I teach mindfulness, I feel I have some insights into which approaches might be helpful.

Below: *Advances in technology have brought us closer to one another in some respects, but may also compound our feelings of isolation.*

- Mindfulness is a life-skill to assist you in dealing better with day-to-day challenges. Some National Health Service departments in the UK offer MBCT training, although so far the courses available to the general public are rather limited. However, the majority of mindfulness courses are conducted privately. Ideally, mindfulness should be a skill training that is provided in healthcare, education, the workplace, and for the Third Age population. Recently, British politicians started to get involved, and some are even studying mindfulness at their workplace.

- We need to emphasize that mindfulness meditation is not merely a technique for coping. If our lifestyle or workplace causes emotional problems, then the mindful response is to change and adapt it (for example, by suggesting proper lunch breaks and a meditation room, or longer holidays, although this might not be a viable option). Thich Nhat Hanh says that a mindful life means not just meditating once a day, but bringing moment-to-moment awareness to every aspect of our life: eating, talking, watering the plants, looking at the clouds, showing concern for others, and so on.

- This all implies that an eight-week course is not sufficient to experience improved mental health, but rather should be seen as "the start" that teaches you skills that need to be applied for the rest of your life. As a society we need to engage in an attitude that supports mindfulness practice as much as it does regular exercise, brushing your teeth, and eating seven portions of fruit and veg a day.

- There is, of course, a danger that mindfulness for the masses will be seen as the panacea for all ills. We need the workplace to take responsibility for its staff and offer "mindfulness at work". But how can an employee apply mindfulness when he feels like a small piece of a jigsaw puzzle? There is a lot of research still to be done, to establish what a mindful workplace might really look like.

- The mental health of all the individuals who make up society is constantly being challenged – we feel under pressure, and no longer have the institutions in place that used to be the first point in calling for help. Very few people know their neighbours or are involved in neighbourhood help schemes. Even fewer people go to church, and many miss out on the support of such communities. The GP who used to make home visits is a thing of the past. And all the technological triggers to which we are exposed during our waking hours cause our brains to experience overload – they are no less harmful in large quantities than tobacco or alcohol.

Mindfulness practice nourishes our ability to learn how to respond wisely, rather than on autopilot and reactively. In the long term, it also points out that certain fundamental conditions that cause us suffering and despair need to be changed and left behind. Thus we are not wrong to see mindfulness as both a political and a socio-economic tool.

Putting down a marker

Mindfulness is a life choice – a marker for any decision we take, a "guideline" by which we live our life. The last verse of the Buddhist metta (or loving-kindness) meditation states: "May all Beings be well, may all Beings be peaceful and free from suffering, may all Beings live at ease and with kindness." If each and every one of us could actually live according to this simple (yet not-so-easy) guideline, so much suffering on our planet could be avoided.

Every one of us is part of the universe expressing itself. Thich Nhat Hanh, said to a child who had asked him why killing was wrong that in fact it is actually impossible to truly kill, because everything and everyone is part of the whole. Nhat Hanh then gave examples: Dr Martin Luther King, Jnr, Mahatma Gandhi, and Jesus were all killed, and yet their deaths made them stay more alive, and spread their message of love and peace further. Nevertheless, if you force a life in its present form to stop – even if it is your own – you cause enormous suffering to those who are left behind.

Write down in your diary what you want to change, withdraw from, or renounce because it actually does not help you. Then write a summary of interventions that would support your well-being in everyday life. Choose one or two, and apply them throughout the day.

Being mindful in everyday life situations

A daily mindfulness practice includes the following:

- Really eating when you eat: seeing the food, its structure, and colours; tasting the texture and the huge number of flavours contained in one mouthful of delicious soup or cake.

- Being truly present when you have a shower, brush your teeth, or shave.

- Using mindful communication when talking to others: listening carefully and responding wisely. Not blowing a fact out of proportion or understating it.

- Bringing awareness to those habits that are depleting you, and which you may want to let go of.

Above: *Bringing increased awareness to how you get from A to B is one aspect of mindful living.*

- Mindfully choosing what you watch on TV and what you read in the newspapers.

- Bringing more awareness to getting from A to B: walking, driving, and travelling mindfully.

- Exploring how it feels to do "chores" mindfully.

- Mindfully looking after yourself and others.

DECKCHAIRS DANCING IN THE BREEZE

This is the story of a young man who met a "lady" on a day out. The beauty of their mindful interaction and their kindness towards each other are a joy to read.

Rosalind was her name; Rosalind Anderton-Butler. As the deckchairs danced in the breeze, the Brighton sunshine smiled upon us equally, making us seem as one. There were two things I understood implicitly: don't ask her name (after all, she's English, I reasoned). It wouldn't be "Rosalind" anyway, not to me, a *total* stranger; it would be "Mrs Anderton-Butler" or maybe even "*Lady* Rosalind" . . . And, for goodness' sake, it's never okay to ask a woman her age.

But I could sort of piece it together – her age, I mean. She set me straight about London during the war, and I could at least deduce which "war" it was. She hadn't yet had children, come the Second World War, but that didn't give me more than a vague age-band. And she regaled me, at intervals, about London in the Swinging Sixties. She must have been a stunner. Her eyes lit up as she remembered her many adventures. Nothing racy, mind you. At least . . . well, that would be telling *tales*, wouldn't it?

I bought us ice-cream cones, and she split her sandwich with me, because "It'd be too much, and there's no point wasting it. Besides, you're too skinny not to eat lunch." Being American, my default setting was to assume that these niceties were the mark of a burgeoning friendship (within twelve minutes I'd be shortening her name to "Ros", wouldn't I?); being English and obviously well bred, she was just being polite, nothing more.

Back to the Eighties, with a snap! I was worried about "playing hookey" from work, but only for a millisecond. Nobody had mobile phones back then (we forget what it was like!), so nobody was going to ring me. If my boss rang up to ask me a question, he'd get an answerphone message from the machine on the left-hand side of my bed. Why, oh why, had I never thought of bunking off work like this before?

I don't really know how it happened, but – suddenly, to my mind – the temperature plummeted. Punctuated by trips to the loo and "Can you watch my things?" from the pair of us, the day just sort of meandered to a natural close. Righting the world's wrongs, we'd talked about *everything* – absolutely everything, it seemed – except for the many no-go subjects, of course. Then she told me she had to be heading back. I offered to accompany her, which she politely declined. "You've eaten a lot today, but you haven't digested very much of it. It's better that you stay here. I know that *this* is why you hopped on today's train to nowhere."

Indeed she was right: en route from Brixton to Green Park, I got off the London Underground prematurely at Victoria, to buy a sandwich and walk through the park to the office. Impulsively, as if somebody else was doing it, I bought a ticket for the next departing train instead. I genuinely didn't care where it went, as long as I could fill my lovelorn lungs with the sea air.

As she inched her way along the wooden planks of the pier and back to the shore, "Lady Rosalind" turned, paused, and smiled a wistful smile, waving goodbye to her inexplicably grateful accomplice.

Despite the intimacy of our exchanges, it never stepped up to "*Do* call me Ros." Indeed, we still hadn't exchanged names, and yet we'd spent the entire *day* sharing secret thoughts: two strangers in deckchairs on Brighton Pier.

MAX EAMES

Mindfulness at work

Each day has the potential for many moments of experience. The more you step out of autopilot mode, the more you will be able to notice the smallest miracle – like seeing the first snowdrop in spring.

Bring awareness to little "miracles" at work too, or even create them yourselves: bring a box of chocolates or a bunch of flowers, and give one to each member of your team.

Start with a positive attitude

While you are at work it can be really useful to have a number of short interventions to hand, which you can fit into any busy schedule.

- Try to see events as they really are, without adding drama or fear to them. If, for example, you are asked to finalize an important peace of work five minutes from now, remember your gentle breathing, ground yourself by feeling your feet firmly connected to the floor, and use the time that you need to finish the task. Deliver it with a smile (or at least with a neutral facial expression). Research shows that smiling changes our internal chemistry for the better (because well-being chemicals are produced). Only do so if you feel it to be congruent with your values, though.

- Try taking a Breathing Space (see page 249) before any meeting that you attend. In this way you can be in the moment for everybody who is participating, including yourself.

- Practise acceptance and compassion: when you find a co-worker challenging, encourage her to talk a little about her life. Maybe ask an invitational question: "What kind of a day you are having today?" Only ask if you are genuinely interested.

Above: *By keeping hydrated at work we create the optimum conditions for efficiency and creativity.*

- Observe your body: every so often scan it a little (see the Body Scan on pages 117–23), checking where you may find tension and discomfort. Then remember to breathe into these areas and release any tension on the out-breath. Drink water regularly, and go for a brief Mindful Walk (see pages 180–1). Your body really needs a little exercise. When washing your hands, you could do a few gentle neck-rolls.

- Download a bell-sound onto your computer, which will remind you to do a short listening practice regularly. You may also want to have some pleasant screensavers, to encourage a brief viewing meditation.

One task at the time

Let the "now" always be your priority. Once you start get worked up about the never-ending number of tasks that need sorting out ("need" is also a mind-construct), you actually trigger chemicals in your body that lead your brain to focus on the "fight or flight" response rather than on creativity. Instead, make it your mission to focus on one single task at a time.

The calmer you are, the less pressure you will feel and the more creative and in-the-flow you will be. Not overloading yourself is a challenge at times like these, when fewer people are paid to do bigger jobs. How can mindfulness help you cope with this extra demand? It can really assist you in being assertive, much better at managing your time, and being honest with your line manager about what you can (or cannot) do.

Some points to remember:

- Learn to recognize how much you can take on, and be honest about it.

- Realize your potential by focusing on one task until it is completed.

- Allow yourself to delegate – find somebody you can train to take on some of the overload. Praise them for their input.

- Learn to be compassionate to yourself and others. Sometimes you may have to say "No" or "Not now, but tomorrow" and, by saying it kindly, honestly, and with your heart, it is more likely to be received with acceptance by the other person.

Responding to pressure and criticism

How can you use mindfulness to deal with pressure and impatience from others, as well as unmanageable

workloads? ADT (Attention Deficit Trait), which is caused by brain overload, is now pandemic in many workplace environments. It manifests in symptoms such as a lack of focus, being easily distracted, and irritation. You may find it very hard to organize your day, stick to your timetable, and set priorities. Your immune system will

Above: *Keeping a bunch of flowers in a vase on your desk can inspire brief "viewing meditations".*

get more and more compromised and may cause you to suffer from an array of ailments, such as flu, respiratory-tract infections, digestive irritations, headaches, and even autoimmune diseases like lupus, fibromyalgia and chronic fatigue syndrome. As you are already barely coping, you may try going to work even when you know you should stay in bed. You will thereby force your system to give you increasing signals of being unwell. Burn-out is the final outcome in many cases.

Here are a few tips that you could benefit from:

- Take regular breaks from your desk and go for a little walk (even going to the loo, washing your hands mindfully, and slowly walking back can act as a "pick-me-up").

- When you drink a cup of tea or coffee, really drink it: feel its shape and surface, notice the temperature, inhale the aroma, and sip the drink with awareness.

- Work as a team. We are pack animals, and acting as part of a team usually helps.

- When you feel criticized, gently allow the content of the criticism to sink in. What can you learn from it and take away for the future? If you feel – after having considered it – that the criticism is unfounded, either share your insights or just let it pass.

- Surround yourself with plants, which can help to improve the air quality indoors, as shown by studies in the *Journal of the American Society for Horticultural Science*. Suitable plants include *Aloe vera*, spider plants, snake plants, golden pothos, chrysanthemums, weeping figs, azaleas, English ivies, bamboo palms, and peace lilies. These are all easy to look after and really do improve air quality. Each plant can, of course, also be used as an object for a "viewing meditation".

MINDFULNESS IN ALL WALKS OF LIFE

There is a time to end the day's work

When you have the confidence and inner strength to know that you have done enough for one day, explain that your load for today is done. It can be challenging when others try to persuade you to do more than you feel able to give right now. A helpful technique is called the "broken record" intervention. Each time a colleague attempts to persuade you to do a little more:

- Breathe mindfully, ground yourself (feeling your feet firmly on the floor), and feel like a mountain or a strong tree.

- Calmly offer a meaningful but unwavering reply: "I think I will be able to focus better tomorrow."

- Like a "broken record", repeat the same answer for as long as it takes for your workmate to accept and understand your decision.

Left: *The "broken record" intervention can be used to make it clear to colleagues that it is time for you to call an end to your day's work.*

CASE STUDY

JONATHAN, 56

I came to mindfulness practice following a significant period of stress and depression, which culminated in my leaving a senior managerial role at work and looking for more fulfilment in my life, where stress, anxiety, and a lack of mindfulness were making me ill. I have found that the practice of mindfulness and compassion has helped me tremendously.

At first this was part of a recovery plan that was based on a Cognitive Behavioural Therapy approach; increasingly it became a learning journey about how to engage with individuals, the environment, people, the world at large (and myself) in a different way. It has involved me learning about how I think, reflect, judge, and criticize – and learning the process of thinking differently – through an eight-week course focusing on stress reduction through Mindfulness-Based Cognitive Therapy, plus several weekend workshops, including work on mindful eating, mindful walking and exercises, and mindful sitting/listening.

Slowly I have succeeded in refocusing the thinking and actions/behaviours acquired and learned over a lifetime – and I currently use this knowledge to take part in group meditation, and individual practice as well. I've come to understand the difference between walking mindfully and taking a mindful walk: I arrive for regular group meditation by taking a mindful walk from the station, up the hill, ready to walk mindfully, little by little, as the first element of my practice.

I can then be ready for a sitting or listening meditation – listening just to the sounds of my own body, or to those in the room or those outside, and not judging, criticizing, or commenting internally on what the sounds are. Just focusing on the sound and putting other thoughts out of my head. I will then be ready for a "metta meditation" – practising loving kindness to myself, to people I love, and to others in the room; to people I do not know well (or hardly at all); to all people, and to all creatures on the Earth, integrating all the practice of the day or evening so far.

Mindfulness has brought me a new way of responding to the challenges I see/throw up in my own world, and has helped me come to terms in life with the deaths of two close family members, and to manage my own recently diagnosed diabetes. I anchor my thinking (sometimes – when I remember to!) in a line from Shakespeare's *Hamlet*: "for there is nothing either good or bad, but thinking makes it so", which takes me back to my own experience in studying the play and seeing it performed onstage several times in my life. I can (and do) integrate that memory, and reflection on it, into my regular meditation practice – which brings me pleasure in acknowledging that I am making progress!

Ageing mindfully

The process of ageing has a difficult place in Western society – we fear the passing of time, looking our age, and, of course, our own mortality.

Ageing well has its own challenges, and it is here that the practice of mindfulness can encourage us to use this phase of life well and with inspiration, or mindlessly fall into a deep hole of desperation and wait for

Below: *Practising mindfulness in later life helps us to embrace life's vicissitudes with an adventurous spirit.*

our last breath. As long as we breathe, we are alive; as long as we are alive, change occurs, and many aspects of this change can turn out to be adventurous, whatever birthday you are approaching.

In a recent documentary on Japan's ageing population (Japan is home to most of the world centenarians) it was sad to think that so many of them are living really mindfully, yet Japan is also the country with the lowest birthrate in the world. There will not be enough taxpayers to continue to cover the present pension rates, and as yet there is no solution to this problem. The BBC documentary, entitled *No Sex Please, We're Japanese* (2013), showed a party of 30 women dancing in cheerleader costumes to American tunes; the youngest participant was in her mid-sixties and the oldest was just over 90. Why is it that we want our parents and grandparents to stay independent and yet we frown upon unusual hobbies or outfits? Who

would want to live to be a hundred if we expect them to lead a boring, hidden life? The motivation of these Japanese women came from realizing that there would be nobody looking after them. They took back their right of independence, and mindfully shared experiences of joy and laughter.

As long as we breathe we are alive; as long as we are alive change occurs.

Ellen Langer: the effect of mindfulness on the elderly

Ellen Langer, a researcher of mindful psychology at Harvard University, writes in an interesting, engaging, and scientific way about mindfulness and mindlessness and the benefits/consequences of each. Her creative way of approaching research has led her to make several long-term studies looking at how mindfulness affects the elderly.

ELSA "DADA" SCHIAPARELLI
AGEING "DISGRACEFULLY"

Elsa Schiaparelli was the second best-known designer in Paris (after Coco Chanel) during the period between the two world wars. She was extremely unusual and deliberately "shocking", and due to her larger-than-life personality most people did not notice that she was only 1.5m (less than 5ft) in height.

The Second World War was like a prison for "fashionistas", as people were focusing on survival rather than on wearing beautiful fashion. But as soon as Paris had recovered after the war, in the early 1950s, Elsa made an unbelievable comeback, at the age of 71. Peggy Guggenheim, Greta Garbo, and Marlene Dietrich were among her most famous customers. Salvador Dalí was a close friend, and Wallis Simpson wore Elsa's design –

a white dress with a red lobster (based on a Dalí painting) – just before she married Edward, Duke of Windsor. For herself, Dada created a "shoe-hat", which she carried off splendidly.

She never lost her desire to provoke, and into her eighties she would never go anywhere (or even watch TV at home) without wearing heavy make-up and a leopard-print outfit. Creativity, inspiration, and believing in herself were the ingredients that fed her spirit and her joy for life, for as long as she lived. She mindfully followed her dream for the rest of her days.

Langer used research studies to demonstrate the effectiveness of mindfulness in helping all people – young and old alike – to become more independent, creative, and healthy. She chose participants living in a nursing home, to ascertain whether independent decision-making would have an impact on their mental and physical health. The experiment included a group who would be encouraged to reconnect to being "their own master", versus a group who continued being "looked after" by staff. The former were guided to make as many decisions themselves as possible. They could choose which clothes to wear; they received the gift of a plant and were encouraged to water it whenever they thought it needed it. The second group also received plants, yet these were looked after by the staff.

The first group could choose whether to see friends and family inside the home or outside (café, cinema, in the rooms of other residents, and so on). They also could choose what to do in the evening: watch a film, play cards, just read. Langer checked the participants' level of happiness, alertness, and activity before and after the experiment. There was a remarkable development in the mindful group, and these residents kept up this enhancement even one-and-a-half years later, when she tested them a second time. They showed more interest and asked more questions in a lecture that they attended, for example.

Their physical well-being had also improved. At the start of the experiment both groups' health evaluations were very similar. One-and-a-half years later the mindful group's health had improved, while the control group's health had declined. The death rate of the first group was half that of the second. Furthermore, mindfulness (everyday mindfulness, rather than practising meditation)

Above: *Mindfulness can help people of all ages to maintain their independence, creativity, and health.*

had also reduced the low mood and depression that often occurs in old age due to a lack of purpose. Memory loss – a problem frequently connected with ageing – had also been improved (and sometimes reversed) by giving these elderly people more responsibilities.

In a second study, in 1981 Ellen Langer and her colleagues drove two groups of men in their seventies and eighties to an ancient monastery in New Hampshire. They turned back the clock and invited the first group of visitors to pretend they were young and living in the 1950s. The second group, who arrived seven days later, were asked just to bring to mind, and focus on, the 1950s. Both groups were surrounded by memorabilia such as 1950s issues of *Life* magazine and newspapers, black-and-white television, and a typical vintage radio.

They were also encouraged to discuss events of the time: Castro's victory-ride into Havana, and the need for bomb shelters during the Cold War, for example. They watched the 1959 film *Anatomy of a Murder* with James Stewart. For the second group it brought back a flood of reminiscences; for the first group it was like watching it for the first time.

The monastery study surprised even Langer's team of researchers. Before and after the experiment, both groups of men took a series of cognitive and physical tests. One week later, dramatic positive changes across the board had already become apparent. Both groups were stronger and more flexible; their height, weight, posture, hearing, vision, and IQ had improved. Their joints were more flexible, their shoulders more squared, their fingers more sensitive and nimble and less contorted by arthritis.

Another important observation was that the men who had acted as if they were actually young showed significantly greater improvement. Those who had "impersonated" younger men seemed to have bodies that actually *were* younger. They were living their lives in the moment of men in their twenties, and that left its stamp upon them.

> "It is not our physical state that limits us ... it is our mindset about our own limits, our perceptions, that does."

So one can deduce that the ageing process is less set in stone than is currently thought. Furthermore, this research has affected not only the field of social psychology, but also that of medicine, psychotherapy, education, business, and sport. "Wherever you put the mind, the body will follow," Langer told a large audience at a recent lecture. "It is not our physical state that limits us . . . it is our mindset about our own limits, our perceptions, that does."

JOURNAL EXERCISE
DON'T ACT YOUR AGE

1 Ask yourself whether you have started "ageing" in an uneventful, monotonous way. Is your life simply a repetitive "Groundhog Day": breakfast, work, lunch, work, dinner, and TV? When you were a young man or woman what were your aspirations, dreams, and goals? What could you start doing right now (or very soon) in order to reconnect with being truly alive?

2 Make a list and share ideas with friends and loved ones. You may inspire them to join you in the "now". It is only now that we are truly alive and have the opportunity to explore.

3 Try not to put this off. Maybe start with something small and easy, and see what happens. Think of people who could serve as inspiration for you.

Langer's definition of mindfulness is a simple recommendation to keep your mind open to possibilities. Mindfulness, she explains, is the process of actively noticing new things, letting go of preconceived mindsets, and then acting on the new observations. This is what she calls "the psychology of possibility . . . we must try new things if we wish to learn and understand them". The famous psychologist Philip Zimbardo claims that Langer "took 'mindfulness' out of Zen and into the bright light of everyday functioning".

On the brink of eternal life

How do you respond to the following statement: the American Academy of Anti-Aging Medicine (A4M), founded in 1993, announced in 2006 at their annual conference, "We are on the verge of practical immortality, with life spans in excess of a hundred years." Do you feel excited and full of expectation, or is the opposite true: do you fear a never-ending, slow decline?

Excitement may only be present when you feel you can offer something to the world and to yourself. People often have a distorted view of what having a "purpose" is. It need not be a huge goal, but rather something that can be achieved. And once you comprehend that there are indeed many things you can learn, master, and enjoy, you may begin to accept that there are many more adventures and experiences ahead.

Finding motivation and inspiration

Time is usually rather more available when you are post-retirement age; on the other hand, some people may have a sense of time running out. What and who inspires you? Think about people who have gone through life-changing experiences and come out the other side stronger and wiser, or simply with zest for more. How can a challenge that might have "crippled" you – whether physically or

MAKE EVERY MOMENT A NEW BEGINNING

Every moment can be precious, if you can incline your mind to perceive it as such. Maybe you can even make it your "purpose" to live, to discover, always to find new and exciting things about life, to start every day afresh and leave yesterday's problems behind.

1 Make a list in your diary of things that are exciting and special about you, no matter how small the list is – and it will definitely be longer than you think! Ask your friends and family to add their insights too.

2 Start with a few examples and add new ones as they come to mind, such as:

- I am creative.
- I am dependable.
- I can adjust things and use them for a purpose that is different from what they were originally designed for (for example, I collect wine-bottle corks and make a memory board out of them; I collect stones and shells from the sea and use them to decorate a vase, vessel, bowl – have you got any other ideas?)
- I am flexible.
- I am tolerant.
- I am caring.
- I am resourceful.

3 Feel free to add some more examples of your own.

MINDFULNESS IN ALL WALKS OF LIFE

emotionally – be the key to discovering something new about yourself? More than once I have read about people who found a great purpose in life only after something "terrible" happened to them – and there is something to be learned from such people.

The psychologists Rick Foster and Greg Hicks call the ability to transform problems and suffering into something meaningful "recasting". When you respond wisely and mindfully to an illness, a chronic condition, the loss of abilities or loved ones, you do not "just get on with it" or "look at the brighter side of life"; first of all, you start by really allowing yourself to feel the magnitude of your ache or loss. Do so without censoring it, and honouring what you *really are aware of*. Only once you get an inkling of true acceptance of what has occurred to you may you compassionately see whether you can "turn the experience round". When you enter your shadowland, can you observe

Above: *A mindful approach to loss means allowing yourself to experience the magnitude of your feelings.*

any opportunities where you can apply what you have learned?

Here are a few people, aged 65–90, who have experienced loss and tribulation and, by mindfully accepting them, may have gained the power to transform themselves decisively, rather than give up.

Judi Dench: "Unless we have a great many laughs . . . along the way, there's no point at all."

John Julius Norwich: "I am very grateful I still have a sense of wonder."

Desmond Tutu: "Dream, dream, dream that we are going to have a world that is incredibly different"

Leonard Cohen: "We are mad in love, and in love we disappear."

Lord Richard Layard: "The key to a good life is harmonious personal relationships."

Susie Orbach: "It's vital to have friends that you can really talk to . . . show them your vulnerability and tell them how you feel."

Bel Mooney: "As I grow older, I become more and more convinced that human kindness is the one power that keeps the world turning."

Robert Mishrahi: "Old age can be a process of opening up . . . and perceiving in yourself the serene, fertile movement of new life."

Having read the above, is there anything you agree with or can apply to yourself? If so, you might want to write it down and devise a plan of action. "Now is the only time to live!"

Discovering joy

Haiku

....

Insects on my face
As the trees wake up
I give them a kiss.

TRISTAN PETTS

Above: *Maintaining a regular connection with others promotes physical and mental well-being as you age.*

This is also the time to give yourself a chance to get pleasure from life – from the little things just as much as from the big things; all joy will strengthen you and, at the same time, give you a sense that life is still attractive. Research shows that people who regularly reconnect to others live longer and stay both physically and mentally alert.

Giving to and helping others is another talent that may well increase your quality of life. It is embedded in "kindness", which is one of the attitudes that tends to develop when you practise MBCT regularly.

It is never too late to experiment with learning new skills:

- Play the piano or any other instrument, or learn a new language.

- Join a choir or theatre society.

- Learn some new dishes to expand your cooking repertoire.

- Engage in a new sport that you can manage physically: t'ai chi, qigong, golf, Pilates, gentle yoga, swimming, walking, mindful movement, dancing.

- Learn new games such as chess, bridge, or something more "out there" – think of some new ideas.

- Join a meditation group to enhance your MBCT practice. There are even "walking meditation groups".

- Get a pet or help out in an animal shelter.

- Experiment with painting, pottery, or sculpture.

- Adopt a grandchild (this is not an official adoption, but refers to older people who would like to help young families who have no family of their own at all, or nearby).

- Go back to university and study a topic you always wanted to know more about. Or attend shorter courses.

Now write down in your diary all the "crazy ideas" that are arising in your awareness. Do not judge them immediately. Just let them sit there, and add to them. Find a couple of friends with whom you can share these thoughts, and who may also be "crazy enough" to join you in your quest for new adventures.

MINDFULNESS IN ALL WALKS OF LIFE

CASE STUDY
THE AUTHOR HERSELF

I always knew, deep in my awareness, that mindfulness existed. As a child, the magical moments when I felt totally connected to Mother Earth were primarily happening in nature.

I recall lying in the grass and sucking on a blade of grass. It tasted a little sour and quite bitter. While being totally content with this "being right here", I observed the softness and coolness of the grass, and that the shorter blades sometimes poked me a little. I watched the sky and clouds above me passing by at different speeds. The cloud formations often looked like figures – some even had faces – and triggered many stories and fantasies, some of which I can still remember. I was surrounded by the smell of evergreens and flowers, which I inhaled with deep gratitude. I was perfectly happy and content.

I know how awareness feels; I recall it well. I also know that it passes and sometimes comes back. Simply allowing it, and turning towards it when it shows up, is "being mindful". Mindfulness is the capacity to deliberately turn your attention to one point of focus – a point of sound, a point of touch, a particular smell, or a combination of these – and experience what life offers, without the need to make it smaller or grander. Accepting what is, and being with it as fully as you possibly can. Each moment of your life is a new beginning. Each moment has potential and can be a vital step towards change or acceptance. So even those tough moments that we'd rather let go of swiftly are part of the tapestry of life's experience, *connecting fully with the life you have now.*

Always seeing life as a gift

Whether you are 18 or 81, you are alive! This is a gift, and it should not be squandered or taken lightly; enjoy the fact that you have a chance to start a different phase of your life now. No matter what you have been through, there is always a way forward. If you live moment by moment you may find it easier to leave the past behind. If you just drop everything and wait for a miracle that will give you your youth back, you may have to wait a very long time.

Just hanging around might be okay occasionally, but getting stuck and listless can lead to depression and addiction (alcohol, food, gambling). If you stop using your muscles they will begin to wither after just two months; once they are weak, you will find it even harder to get around and will feel even more stuck. So although I highly promote "being in the moment" (Yin), you also need to be fully alive (Yang) in order to enjoy those decades that give you the freedom to be your own master.

The German monk Father Anselm Green, who wrote *The Art of Growing Older*, says that ageing can be compared to the four seasons. Spring symbolizes childhood and youth. Summer shines brightly with the sense of being an independent adult who can, if he or she chooses, create a life full of adventure. Autumn, on the other hand, creates new colours and smells in nature, with the sun shining less harshly, and is the time for harvesting and reaping, but also for trying new things, now that you may have fewer responsibilities (for example, towards bringing up children or making a career). Winter has its own beauty: there is peace, quietness, and an invitation to slow down your pace. Yet it is also filled with possibilities: building snowmen outside or sitting in front of an open fire, telling stories or simply "being alive".

CASE STUDY

LILO, 67

It is January 2008. I go for a psychotherapy session, but after hearing the counsellor speak of mindfulness, I come away feeling an immediate reconnection with another part of myself, which has mostly lain dormant in the years of rushing to full-time work, of bringing up children, having a relationship, and family demands.

The reconnection is very simple: STOPPING and BEING IN THE MOMENT. Any moment – each moment – no matter what comes into the mind: being with pain, anguish, tears, screams, fury, hurt, hate, and . . . love. Being with myself in all this, not running away into distraction, not kidding myself, but facing myself with quiet acceptance and kindness, offers release, a letting go, being in the moment.

As the single gong-sound rings out, it feels as though I am being gently pulled back into a feeling state I have always known since childhood, as I enter my own stillness, centred in my breath . . . breathing slowly in and slowly out, an inner part of me reconnected to all beyond my own skin, bringing such peacefulness, such well-being, and such love.

MINDFULNESS IN ALL WALKS OF LIFE

A chance for growth and wisdom

The next story focuses on illness and the realization that even when recovery occurs – thank God – we are still susceptible to ageing.

When we can approach the final decades of our life with interest, curiosity, and compassion, every day will offer itself as an opportunity for growth and wisdom.

CASE STUDY
GARY, 65

For me, mindfulness is about engaging with life, particularly when it gets rough. "Fortunately", life has given me a number of opportunities to practise this, especially when I got a potentially terminal type of cancer, nearly 20 years ago. But, even with the everyday events of life, there are plenty of difficulties and plenty of reasons to practice mindfulness.

I was diagnosed with non-Hodgkin lymphoma in 1995. At the time I had a young family and, unfortunately, as my type of NHL was rare, my oncologist could not say what the prognosis was, other than that it was serious and potentially terminal. It was a dreadful time, both for me and my family.

I had a real need for stillness when the cancer hit me. However, while I had done some meditation prior to my cancer – yoga and a year or so of Zen meditation – I wasn't a regular meditator at the time, and that made it hard to practise, given the anxiety that I was experiencing after diagnosis, and during and after treatment. I did manage to cope, particularly using qigong, but mindfulness training would have made a real difference, had it been widely available in those days in the UK.

Following my initial cancer treatment and a recurrence, I continued to have problems with anxiety, and to worry about another recurrence. So when I discovered mindfulness at the end of 2001, it was a revelation. And it wasn't just mindfulness – it was also meditation, a daily practice; and, for the first time in my life, I found a way that allowed me to cope with life, whatever hit me. And now, after more than 12 years, I continue to practise daily both formal meditation and using mindfulness in my daily life. It really works for me, every day! And it's constantly developing and deepening: that ability to work fluidly with, and to learn from, life's experiences. And mindfulness is the core.

I was interested in teaching mindfulness generally, but I knew at the time that my focus was always going to be on cancer; and indeed that has been the case. Initially I taught a five-week introductory course on mindfulness and cancer, with an experienced colleague, at a London cancer-support centre.[7] Since the start of 2013 I have been teaching a full eight-week mindfulness course at the centre and at St George's Hospital, in Tooting.

One wonderful lesson coming out of the "Mindfulness for Cancer" courses that I've been teaching is that suffering is universal – whether one has cancer or is just dealing with the stresses of everyday life. However, our courses also provide an underlying model for how mindfulness supports the transition from the crisis of an initial diagnosis, through everyday mindfulness, to seeing the meaning of one's experience.

Not surprisingly, this approach to mindfulness can have tremendous value in dealing with ageing, and the inevitable changes and losses that accompany it. Mindfulness can teach us skilfully how to be with ourselves and our experience as we age, even as we confront the reality that we simply cannot do the things we used to be able to do. With this in mind, I co-founded three years ago a group called Insightful Ageing, aimed at those who are 50 and older. We meet monthly and, supported by all in the group, examine our lives mindfully.

Albert Einstein shared the following with us:

"If one is at peace with the mind, one can sit in the middle of a prison riot with little or no concern. However, if one is at war with the mind, then even if one sits in a cave it will seem as if one is in the middle of a prison riot. It is the stillness of the mind that brings a peace within."

and:

"A human being is part of the whole, called by us the 'Universe'; a part limited in time and space. He experiences himself, his thoughts, and feelings, as something separated from the rest, a kind of optical delusion of his consciousness. This delusion is a kind of prison for us, restricting us to our personal desires and to affection for a few persons nearest to us. Our task must be to free ourselves from this prison by widening our circle of compassion to embrace all living creatures and the whole of nature in its beauty."

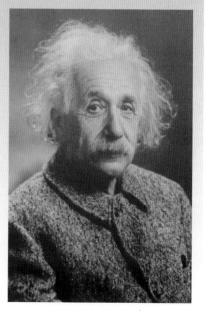

A MOST WONDERFUL SPIRIT WITH AN UNRELIABLE BODY

Jaynie Pigford is blessed with a fantastically creative brain and with open, compassionate love. Her body, however, has been failing her since her early thirties, when she developed a serious autoimmune disease. She writes: "I ended up in hospital for seven months with a catalogue of lupus-related disasters and much dancing with death.

With pneumonia and blood clots all over my body, I had the time and desperation to start regular mindfulness practice . . . I learned that if I observed horrendous pain, it became more tolerable. At one point, on the verge of death, I felt peace, open-heartedness, a sense of connectedness, and absolute awe at our world. There was only the moment."

Opposite is one of her poems, which is deeply moving and enlightening.

An Ode to
Dr Death

You make me sick.
Prowling in the shadows
With your glistening knife,
Smirking and taunting
'Cause you can just snip
My string of life.
I hate you! I hate you . . .
You cold, indifferent, sadistic . . .
. . . and yet I wonder . . .
Without you, would I bother to see
The dandelion's clock of perfect stars?
Would I feel the dusk of misty
    morning
Or connect with those
Whose string you also threaten?
Ah, Dr Death, you make me smile.
Come on, snarl, sneer, brandish
    your knife.
All you're going to do
Is make me dance with the beauty
    of Life!

JAYNIE PIGFORD

The Lady in Number 6: how music saved my life

I have met several people who had extraordinary energy and presence. Unfortunately I did not manage to meet Alice Herz-Sommer in the flesh, but I have seen a number of interviews with her. She passed away at the age of 110, the oldest Holocaust survivor. Thankfully, the latest documentary about her life, *The Lady in Number 6*, won an Oscar for the Best Short Documentary in 2014; she died a week before the award was granted, but I am convinced it would not have made any difference to her life.

Alice believed in, and acted according to, her belief that *good* was her guidance. Please watch the documentary, which captured her unbelievable inner strength and beauty. She lived mostly for her music

Below: *Holocaust survivor Alice Herz Sommer was an embodiment of mindfulness and compassion.*

(she was a pianist and music teacher), which made her happy, even in Theresienstadt concentration camp. She said that as long as she could play her piano, things could not be all bad. But she also loved other human beings: she adored having visitors and communicating with them. She also said that she remembered everything that was beautiful, and did not believe in complaining: "Hatred eats the soul of the hater; I know about the bad, but I focus on the good." She was not deluded. Her mind was sharp and stayed so until the end. She practised three hours of piano-playing every day.

Even when her son died at the age of 64 (and he had survived the concentration camp with her) Alice focused on the positive aspects. She shared that he did not have to suffer pain, and that he died peacefully. She had understood the essence of mindfulness and compassion.

A final piece of counsel (from the heart)

Remember that every moment has the potential to be special. The tiny frog in the grass, the giggling child, the delicious heavenly tea, waking up every morning – all this – and much more – is a miracle, because it is how life expresses itself.

All you need to do is actually see it.

Practising formal meditation regularly

Remember that mindfulness is not a sticking plaster. It will only assist you in tackling your problems if it becomes part of your regular life. So:

- Create a special place for meditation.

- Make sure you pencil in regular dates with yourself to meditate.

- Be kind and don't judge yourself when you lapse or forget to practise.

- Remember that every moment is a new beginning.

- Don't forget: there is no right or wrong way of meditating, but only *your* way of doing so.

- Remember that the rest of your life is the time you can use to meditate.

- Perhaps join a meditation group, or invite friends and family to join you in your meditation practice.

Notes

1. S Lazar et al., *Psychiatric Research: Neuroimaging* 191 (2011), pp.36–43.

2. Rick Hanson, *Buddha's Brain* (New Harbinger, 2009), p.37.

3. See Michael Chaskalson's book *The Mindful Workplace* (Wiley-Blackwell, 2011), p.75, re the "happiness set-point" and damage to the left versus right pre-frontal cortex and the effect on mood.

4. For further information, check out: R J Davidson, J Kabat-Zinn et al., "Alterations in brain and immune function produced by mindfulness meditation", *Psychosomatic Medicine* 65, pp.564–70.

5. On the importance of this study for an ageing population, see S W Lazar, C E Kerr, R H Wasserman et al., "Meditation experience is associated with increased cortical thickness", *Neuroreport* 16 (17), (2005), pp.1893–7.

6. For the last three studies, see the *Journal of Alternative and Complementary Medicine* 9 (3), pp.355–69.

7. Paul's Cancer Support Centre, 20–22 York Road, London SW11 3QA; tel: 020 7924 3924; www.paulscancersupportcentre.org.uk

Glossary

acceptance
To become fully aware of difficulties and respond to them with care rather than thoughtless reaction.

adrenal glands
Glands that release stress-response hormones directly into the bloodstream; part of the body's endocrine system.

adrenaline
A stress-response neurotransmitter hormone secreted by the adrenal glands in response to fight-or-flight stimuli. *See also* "fight or flight" response; cortisol.

amygdala
The control and response centre in the brain, which switches on the "fight or flight" response and plays a key role in the expression of emotions. *See also* "fight or flight" response; limbic system.

anchors of attention
An object or thought on which attention is focused during meditation.

antidepressant
Medication to treat conditions including depression, anxiety disorders, and some personality disorders. Antidepressant drugs include selective serotonin reuptake inhibitors (SSRIs) and serotonin-norepinephrine reuptake inhibitors (SNRIs), which affect the brain's uptake of seratonin, a good-mood chemical. See also depression; serotonin.

Attention Deficit Trait (ADT)
A response to the brain being overwhelmed with information; symptoms include distraction and irritation. "Brain overload".

autoimmune disease
A disorder in which the body mistakenly attacks its healthy cells; conditions include lupus, fibromyalgia, and chronic fatigue syndrome.

autopilot mode
A mindless state in which we perform familiar rituals without being fully conscious of our actions. *See also* mindlessness.

body scan
A key mindfulness practice during which we focus attention on each part of the body slowly, as a way of becoming present within the mind, body, and moment.

borderline personality disorder (BPD)
A pattern of behaviour that is often characterized by emotional instability and intense emotions that negatively affect relationships and self-esteem. *See also* depression; personality disorder.

Buddhism
Belief system based on the teachings of Siddhartha Gautama, the Buddha or "awakened one". Aspects of mindfulness are influenced by Buddhist approaches and practices: meditation; awareness of our thoughts; and being in the present moment, for example.

burnout
Exhaustion due to long-term stress.

choiceless awareness
A free-flowing, non-judgemental response to sensory impressions during meditation. Also known as spacious awareness.

cognitive function
The psychological function of the brain; the processing of thoughts and emotions.

cerebral cortex
A fine layer of neural tissue surrounding the brain that sends and receives sensory information around different areas of the brain.

compassion
The ability to suffer with others with respect and kindness for them.

cortisol
A stress-response neurotransmitter hormone released during the fight or flight response. See also "fight or flight" response.

depression
A condition associated with symptoms such as low mood, anxiety, negative thoughts, lack of motivation, and poor self-care; it may be a triggered by life events, such as trauma and bereavement, or change, such as menopause or childbirth; for some people, depression can be a symptom of a long-term psychiatric issue. See also antidepressant; serotonin.

electromyogram (EMG)
A visual-display record showing the effect of neurological activity on muscle cells in the body. Electrodes are inserted into the muscle tissue through the skin or placed on top of the skin to monitor activity.

endorphins
Feel-good chemicals – the body's natural opiates that are released to decrease pain and stress and give a sense of euphoria after exercise, for example.

expanding awareness
Extending the attention from the breath to the body, and to thoughts and feelings during meditation.

"fight or flight" response
The amygdala's reaction to perceived threat, resulting in the release of cortisol, blood sugar, and adrenaline. See also amygdala; adrenaline; cortisol.

fMRI scanner
Functional Magnetic Resonance Imaging scanner that allows us to see the conscious and unconscious processes of the brain in response to stress and during meditation.

Four Mantras
Four affirmations designed by Vietnamese monk and mindfulness educator Thich Nhat Hanh to avoid destructive emotions in relationships: 1. "Darling, I am here for you." 2. "Darling, I know you are there." 3. "Darling, I know you suffer." 4. "Darling, I suffer (because of you) and I truly try to practise compassion and forgiveness. Please help me do this for us."

Gestalt Therapy
A type of psychotherapy that focuses on the experience of the present moment and individual freedom and responsibility.

groundedness
A feeling of security when we are fully present to our body.

hippocampus
Area of the brain associated with long-term memories and assigning emotional value to memories; the store-house of our past experiences. *See also* limbic system.

limbic system
Collection of brain structures thought to be vital in the perception and the expression of emotions; contains the hippocampus and the amygdala.

meditation
A practice that aims to change the state of the mind to benefit the whole person. Often the objective is to feel a sense of relaxation, and/or create conditions for the unconscious mind to be expressed.

metta
Loving-kindness.

metta meditation
Practising loving-kindness towards yourself and those you know and do not know.

mindful breathing
Breathing with full attention on the process and sensations of breathing.

mindful movement
An awareness of the sensations of the body during gentle movement, bringing body and mind together.

mindful walking practice
A key mindfulness practice in which we walk to a destination with full awareness of what we are doing; the focus is on being present to our experience during the walk. *See also* walking meditation.

mindfulness
Experiencing life with full attention and an awareness of the present moment.

mindlessness
A lack of attention and awareness of the present moment. *See also* autopilot mode.

negative automatic thoughts (NATs)
Habitual negative thinking that prevents us from experiencing the present moment without judgement.

nervous system
Comprises the central nervous system (containing the brain and spinal cord) and peripheral nervous system (a system, mainly comprised of nerves, which connect the central nervous system to the rest of the body). The nervous system is responsible for whole-body communication. *See also* parasympathetic nervous system; sympathetic nervous system.

neurons
Nerve cells that transmit information to other cells in the body.

neurotransmitters
Chemicals released in response to signals from neurons; "messenger" chemicals. *See also* neurons.

noradrenaline
A stress-response neurotransmitter hormone activated by stress and "fight or flight". *See also* "fight or flight" response; cortisol; adrenaline.

obsessive-compulsive behaviour
An anxiety disorder characterized by unwanted, intrusive thoughts, rituals, and other behaviours.

one-on-one therapy
Individual therapy.

open awareness
Being present in the moment and aware of your thoughts in an open, non-judgemental way.

oxytocin
A "bonding" hormone associated with empathy and intimacy.

parasympathetic nervous system (PSNS)
The part of the nervous system that signals the body to rest and relax. *See also* nervous system.

personality disorder
A condition marked by disturbed behaviour perceived as socially unacceptable. *See also* borderline personality disorder; depression.

raisin exercise
A key mindful eating practice in which we learn to fully experience and appreciate eating and tasting.

randomized control trial (RCT)
Research in which individuals are chosen at random to receive the different treatments being studied in the trial.

self-compassion
Applying compassion to ourselves; self-empathy. *See also* compassion

serotonin
The body's natural "happiness" chemical, used also in many antidepressant drugs. *See also* antidepressant.

Siddhartha Gautama (The Buddha)
See Buddhism.

spacious awareness
See choiceless awareness.

sympathetic nervous system (SNS)
The part of the nervous system that stimulates the fight-or-flight response. *See also* "fight or flight" response; nervous system.

Taoism
A belief system and influencer of mindfulness practice, Taoist emphases include the wisdom of our intuition, letting go of inner attachments, and the importance of being in the present moment. The "Tao" indicates inner authority, the need to be lead by the self rather than society's conventions.

visualization
Generating positive mental images, usually during meditation.

walking meditation
Walking without a destination so we focus on the movement of the body, and become observers of ourselves walking. *See also* mindful walking practice.

Reading list

Core reading

Books followed by * are highly recommended.

Baer, R E, *Mindfulness-Based Treatment Approaches, A Clinician's Guide* (Academic Press, 2005).

Collard, P, *Journey into Mindfulness: Gentle ways to let go of stress and live in the moment* (Octopus Books, 2013).

Collard, P, *MBCT for Dummies* (John Wiley, 2013).

Collard, P, *The Little Book of Mindfulness: 10 Minutes a Day to Less Stress, More Peace* (Octopus Books, 2014).

Collard, P, *Mindfulness for Compassionate Living: Mindful ways to less stress and more kindness* (Gaia, 2014).

Crane, R S, *Mindfulness-Based Cognitive Therapy* (Routledge, 2008) *.

Kabat-Zinn, J, *Full Catastrophe Living: Using the Wisdom of Your Body and Mind to Face Stress, Pain, and Illness* (Delta, 1990) *.

Kabat-Zinn, J, *Mindfulness Meditation for Everyday Life* (Piatkus, 2001).

Kabat-Zinn, J, *Coming to Our Senses: Healing Ourselves and the World Through Mindfulness* (Piatkus, 2005).

Santorelli, S, *Heal Thy Self: Lessons on Mindfulness in Medicine* (Bell Tower, 1999).

Segal, Z V, Williams, J M G, and Teasdale, J D, *Mindfulness-Based Cognitive Therapy for Depression: A New Approach to Preventing Relapse* (Guilford Press, 2002) *.

Williams, J M G, Segal, Z V, Teasdale, J D, and Kabat-Zinn, J, *The Mindful Way through Depression* (Guilford Press, 2007) *.

Other suggested titles

The following is not intended to be a comprehensive list.

Batchelor, S and M, *Meditation for Life* (Frances Lincoln, 2001).

Bien, T, *Mindful Therapy* (Wisdom Publications, 2006).

Chodren, P, *When Things Fall Apart: Heart Advice for Difficult Times* (Shambala, 2000).

Epstein, M, *Thoughts Without a Thinker: Psychotherapy from a Buddhist Perspective* (Basic Books, 1996).

Epstein, M, *Going to Pieces Without Falling Apart: A Buddhist perspective on wholeness* (Broadway reprint, 1999).

Germer, C K, Siegel, R D, and Fulton, P R, *Mindfulness and Psychotherapy* (Guilford Press, 2005).

Gilbert, P, *Compassion: Conceptualisations, Research and Use in Psychotherapy* (Brunner-Routledge, 2005).

Goldstein, J, *Insight Meditation: The Practice of Freedom* (Shambala, 2003).

Goldstein, J, and Kornfield, J, *Seeking the Heart of Wisdom: The Path of Insight Meditation* (Shambala, 1987).

Goleman, D (ed.), *Healing Emotions: Conversations with the Dalai Lama on Mindfulness, Emotions and Health* (Shambala, 2003).

Goleman, D (ed.), *Destructive Emotions: A Dialogue with the Dalai Lama* (Bloomsbury, 2004).

Hayes, S, *Get Out of Your Mind and Into Your Life (a self-help manual of Acceptance and Commitment Therapy)* (New Harbinger, 2005).

Hayes, S, Follette, V, and Linehan, M (ed.), *Mindfulness and Acceptance: Expanding the cognitive behavioural tradition* (Guilford Press, 2004).

Hayes, S, and Strosahl, K D (ed.), *A Practical Guide to Acceptance and Commitment Therapy* (Guilford Press, 2005).

Heaversedge, J, and Halliwell, E, *The Mindful Manifesto* (Hay House, 2012).

Kabat-Zinn, J and M, *Everyday Blessings: The Inner Work of Mindful Parenting* (Hyperion, 1998).

Kornfield, J, *A Path with Heart: A guide through the promises and perils of spiritual life* (Rider, 1994).

Kornfield, J, and Feldman, C, *Soul Food: Stories to Nourish the Spirit and the Heart* (HarperCollins, 1996).

Lazar, S W, Kerr, C E, Wasserman, R H, et al., "Meditation experience is associated with increased cortical thickness", *Neuroreport* 16 (17), (2005), pp.1893–7.

Linehan, M M, *Skills Training Manual for Treating Borderline Personality Disorder* (Guilford Press, 1993).

Ma, S H, and Teasdale, J D, "Mindfulness-Based Cognitive Therapy for depression: Replication and exploration of differential relapse prevention effects", *Journal of Consulting and Clinical Psychology* 70, (2002), pp.278–87.

Nhat Hanh, T, 1991, *The Miracle of Mindfulness* (Rider).

Rosenberg, L, *Breath By Breath: The Liberating Practice of Insight Meditation* (Shambala, 2004).

Salzberg, S, *A Heart as Wide as the World: Living with Mindfulness, Wisdom and Compassion* (Shambala, 1997).

Useful websites

The following is not intended to be a comprehensive list.

http://www.bangor.ac.uk/mindfulness
The Centre for Mindfulness Research and Practice (CMRP) at Bangor University, Wales

http://www.entermindfulness.com
Website for Dr Patrizia Collard's MBCT coaching and therapy practice

http://bemindful.co.uk
Website providing an online course to reduce anxiety, depression and stress

http://www.mindfulnet.org
Website containing extensive information related to mindfulness

https://www.mindsightinstitute.com
Institute linking science to practical applications for cultivating mindfulness skills

http://franticworld.com
Website of Danny Penman, award-winning journalist and mindfulness author

http://www.mentalhealth.org.uk
Website of the UK's Mental Health Foundation

http://www.breathworks-mindfulness.org.uk
Organization offering courses on mindfulness to overcome stress and promote health

http://www.stressminus.co.uk
Website for Dr Patrizia Collard's mindfulness workshops

http://pvfhk.org/index.php/en
Website of the Asian Institute of Applied Buddhism

http://www.umassmed.edu/cfm
University of Massachusetts Medical School's Centre for Mindfulness

http://www.mindfulschools.org
Courses for adults to learn mindfulness and use it with young people

Index